SLAVES I

Claiborne County Mississippi

Brenda Terry

HERITAGE BOOKS
2010

HERITAGE BOOKS
AN IMPRINT OF HERITAGE BOOKS, INC.

Books, CDs, and more—Worldwide

For our listing of thousands of titles see our website at
www.HeritageBooks.com

Published 2010 by
HERITAGE BOOKS, INC.
Publishing Division
100 Railroad Ave. #104
Westminster, Maryland 21157

Copyright © 1995 Brenda Terry

All rights reserved. No part of this book may be reproduced or transmitted in any form or by any means, electronic or mechanical, including photocopying, recording or by any information storage and retrieval system without written permission from the author, except for the inclusion of brief quotations in a review.

International Standard Book Numbers
Paperbound: 978-0-7884-0269-2
Clothbound: 978-0-7884-8425-4

WORD FROM THE AUTHOR

The information contained in this book was not only compiled and formatted to aid in locating Slavery Ancestry, but also early White Settlers of Mississippi.

I conduct my research with the attitude that every name is important and I may save some dedicated Family Historian years of research if I take care to note anything that may be of aid to someone else. In exercising this belief, I have indexed this book by Slave's first name, and Owner's last name. I have listed relations to Slaves, and relations to Owners. I've personally shared the frustration of having a hot trail that leads to a sea of confusion or a dead end that can last for months or years. If this book can aid in the discovery of one ancestor, the resources spent in making this information available to you were well worth it.

Brenda Terry

January 31, 1995

TABLE OF CONTENTS

INTRODUCTION. v

HISTORY. vi

I. Names From Willbook 1

II. Names from Port Gibson
Property List. 53

III. Names from Certificate of
Slaves for Sale. 125

IV. Willbook Witnesses. 169

V. Willbook Additional Names. 179

INDEX 181

BIBLIOGRAPHY 195

INTRODUCTION

This work consists of data compiled from Wills, Property Lists, and Certificate for Slave Sale from the Claiborne County Courthouse located in Port Gibson, Mississippi.

Chapter I consists of an easy to read format from Will Book A. The dates of these Wills range from October 1804 through May 1833. The names are sequenced by slaves's first name and contains the owners name, date the will was written, owners heirs, heir's relationship to owner, will page, slave's spouse, children and siblings if applicable. There are also notes that were observed to be possibly useful in aiding the researcher.

The data in Chapter II data was compiled from the "Port Gibson Property List 1846-1858". I found this book by chance while rummaging among the many forgotten records in the courthouse. The wives in Port Gibson owned property separate from their husbands and were required to report this property. This data was formatted containing owner's names, slave's first name, age and dates.

Chapter III lists data extracted from "Certificate for Slave Sale" contained also in the "Port Gibson Property List 1846-1858". Here I found slaves purchased in Missouri, Kentucky, and Tennessee, and taken to Claiborne County to be sold. This chapter contains the trader's name, slave's name, age if applicable and originating county and state.

HISTORY

Mississippi Territory was formed in 1798 by the U.S. Congress. There were only two significant regions of settlement, the Natchez District found in the southern part of the state along the Mississippi River, and the St. Stephens District in the eastern section on the Tombigbee River. Early settlers moved onto lands that were previously owned by the Choctaw, Creek and the Chickasaw tribes. The acquisition of this land was through land grant distribution from the Treaty of Paris in 1783 and Pinckney Treaty of 1795.[1]

The migration of settlers to this area were so in numbers, that by 1817 the territory became a state in 1817, with a population of about 40,000 Whites and 30,000 African-Americans.[2] The southern quarter and a narrow strip up the Mississippi to the Yazoo were open to Legal Settlement. The rest of the state was held by the Chickasaw and Choctaw Nations. In 1832, through treaties made with the Choctaw and Chickasaw, all land in the present state of Mississippi was opened for settlement. Mississippi became known as the "Cotton King" years before the Civil War, aided by the labors of hundred of thousands of slaves.

In Mississippi there were, in 1860, 353,899 Whites and 437,404 African-American, of whom less than 1,000 were free. This number was small since manumission was not popular, even before the state was developed. They reached

---

[1] Rowland Dunbar,"Mississippi, The Heart of the South",p.381, VOL I.
[2] Vernon Lane Warton,"The Negro in Mississippi 1865-1890,p.10.

HISTORY

their greatest number about 1840, when the Census listed 1,336 and declined steadily numbering only 775 in 1860. There were 255 in Adams County alone. In 1860, 601 of the 773 slaves were mulattoes and lived in town. Of the 437,404 slaves, the great majority lived in the plantation counties. They were owned by 30,943 slaveholders, who possessed an average of 14.1 slaves each, but of whom only about 6,000 owned more than the average number.[4] The population had only been a few thousand at the beginning of the century and small in 1820.

Then from 1840 on, the Cotton Kingdom spread over Mississippi, greatly increasing its population. The result was that after the war, there was in this state a group of planters whose great plantations dominated the rich Black Belt. From Memphis to the gulf were a succession of counties with 60 percent or more of African-American population.[5]

Claiborne County is located on the Mississippi river in the southwestern part of the state, and constituted a part of old Natchez District which was settled by the French, Spaniards, English and Americans during the eighteenth century. The First General Assembly, Second Session of 1801-02 passed a number of measures by which the territory was divided into five counties on January 11, 1802.

The name of the Pickering County of 1799 was

[4]Vernon Lane Warton,"The Negro in Mississippi 1865-1890",p.10
[5]Rowland, Dunbar,"Mississippi, The Heart of the south",p.534

HISTORY

Jefferson and Claiborne extended eastward to the western bank of Pearl River. North of the dividing line was Claiborne County, named in the honor of the new Governor, William Charles Cole Claiborne of Sussex County Virginia. On June 29, 1822, the boundaries between Claiborne and Warren Counties (the home of Jefferson Davis) were defined. The first civil officers of the county, commissioned January 30, 1802, were William Downs, G. W. Humphreys, James Stansfield, Ebenezer Smith and Daniel Winch, Justice of the Peace; Samual Cobwin, Sheriff; Matthew Teirney, Clerk; Samual Gibson, Coroner.[6]

The towns of Grand Gulf, Brandywine and Buckland were prosperous settlements in the early part of the Nineteenth Century.

Grand Gulf was the shipping point on the river for Port Gibson, and as late as 1858 had 1,000 to 1,500 inhabitants. Port Gibson is the county seat of Claiborne county, and is a city on the Yazoo and Mississippi Valley R. R., 29 miles south of Vicksburg and 40 miles northeast of Natchez. It is 20 miles from the mouth of Bayou Pierre, at a point where the old Natchez Trace crossed that stream. Settlers moved in during the early 1770's, Lyman's Mandamus on the Big Black and the Bayou Pierre dates from 1775.

Samuel Gibson laid out the original townsite in 1788. The beautiful old town of Port Gibson

[6]Rowland Dunbar,"Mississippi, The Heart of the South",p.534

HISTORY

is the town Grant said "was to beautiful to burn". The court house that was erected in 1839, by William H. Faulkner And George Stockdill still stands and was spared during the Civil War even though Port Gibson was the scene of much hard fighting while Grant was forcing his way to Vicksburg.[7]

[7]Rowland Dunbar,"Mississippi, The Heart of the South",p.381

NAMES FROM WILLBOOK

```
Name     : Abraham           Owner: Durbin, Daniel
Date     : 1822/03/05        Page : 200
Bequeath : Durbin, Elizabeth
Relation : Wife

Name     : Abraham           Owner: White, Thomas
Date     : 1803/02/18        Page : 008
Bequeath : White, Sarah
           White, Thomas
Relation : Wife & Son

Name     : Abram             Owner: Barnes, Esther
Date     : 1831/10/05        Page : 288
Bequeath : Barnes, Elias
Relation : Son

Name     : Abram             Owner: Brashears,
                                    Turner
Date     : 1833/05/30        Page : 276
Bequeath : Breashears, Joseph
Relation : Son

Name     : Abram             Owner: Brisco, Thomas
Date     : 1832/04/18        Page : 232
Bequeath : Brisco, Claiborne
Relation : Son

Name     : Abram             Owner: Daniel, Ann
Date     : 1830/07/26        Page : 218
Bequeath : Tugg, Margaret
Relation : Daughter

Name     : Adam              Owner: Gibson, Samual
Date     : 1817/11/24        Page : 079
Bequeath : Gibson, Rebecca
Relation : Daughter

Name     : Affey             Owner: Gibson, Clark
Date     : 1820/01/23        Page : 088
Bequeath : Clark, Elijah
Relation : Son
Note     : Affey was bequeathed to
           Elijah Clark's Children.
```

NAMES FROM WILLBOOK

Name   : Aggy   Owner: Watts, Nancy
Date   : 1831/04/12   Page : 266
Note: Nancy Watts was Aggy's grandmother.
           Nancy was also a free woman of color.

Name   : Albert   Owner: Daniel, Ann
Date   : 1830/07/26   Page : 218
Bequeath: Watkins, Lary
Relation: Daughter

Name   : Albert   Owner: Green, Abram
Date   : 1826/06/02   Page : 168
Bequeath: Green, Martha
Relation: Daughter

Name   : Albert   Owner: Wooldridge, W.H.
Date   : 1810/04/18   Page : 053
Bequeath: Wooldridge, Elam
Relation: Son

Name   : Alexander   Owner: Bullock, Mary
Date   : 1833/05/17   Page : 273
Parents : Billy and Patty
Siblings: Jim, Flora, Tenach, Rhoda,
           New, Vira, Melinda and
           Sarah.
Note   : Alexander was emancipated and
           sent to Libera.

Name   : Alfred   Owner: Crane, Waterman
Date   : 1829/02/05   Page : 149
Bequeath: Young, Clarissa
Relation: Daughter

Name   : Allen   Owner: Brashears,
                                 Turner
Date   : 1833/05/30   Page : 276
Bequeath: Brashears, Amelia
Relation: Daughter

Name   : Ally   Owner: Hanna, James
Date   : 1826/07/11   Page : 160
Bequeath: Robinson, Ann
Relation: Sister

NAMES FROM WILLBOOK

Name   : Alphnea   Owner: Brashears,
                                   Turner
Date   : 1833/05/30   Page : 276
Bequeath: Brashears, Joseph
Relation: Son

Name   : Anderson   Owner: Green, Abram
Date   : 1826/06/02   Page : 168
Bequeath: Green, Martha
Relation: Daughter

Name   : Ann   Owner: Brashears,
                                   Turner
Date   : 1833/05/30   Page : 276
Bequeath: Brashears, Amelia
Relation: Daughter

Name   : Ann   Owner: Crane, Waterman
Date   : 1829/02/05   Page : 149
Bequeath: Crane, Catherine
Relation: Wife
Parents : Isaac and Mill.
Siblings: Charles, Mary Joe.

Name   : Ann   Owner: Thompson, John
Date   : 1833/03/30   Page : 290
Bequeath: Thompson, Myra
          Thompson, Sophia
Relation: Daughters

Name   : Annace   Owner: Durbin, Daniel
Date   : 1822/03/05   Page : 200
Bequeath: Durbin, Elizabeth
Relation: Wife

Name   : Anney   Owner: Moors, Robert
Date   : 1817/02/18   Page : 076
Bequeath: Moors, William
Relation: Son

Name   : Arab   Owner: Brashears,
                                   Turner
Date   : 1833/05/30   Page : 276
Bequeath: Brashears, Joseph

NAMES FROM WILLBOOK

Arab(cont)
Relation: Son

Name   : Arena   Owner: Wooldridge, W.H.
Date   : 1810/04/18   Page : 053
Bequeath: Wooldridge, Elam
Relation: Son

Name   : Ariann   Owner: Durbin, Daniel
Date   : 1822/03/05   Page : 200
Bequeath: Durbin, Elizabeth
Relation: Wife

Name   : Aristide   Owner: Durbin, Daniel
Date   : 1822/03/05   Page : 200
Bequeath: Durbin, Elizabeth
Relation: Wife

Name   : Armsted   Owner: Thompson, John
Date   : 1833/03/30   Page : 290
Bequeath: Thompson, Myra
           Thompson, Sophia
Relation: Daughters

Name   : Beck   Owner: Clark, Gibson
Date   : 1820/01/23   Page : 088
Bequeath: Clark, Susanah
Relation: Granddaughter

Name   : Ben   Owner: Barnes, Joseph
Date   : 1821/04/08   Page : 134
Bequeath: Barnes, Susan
Relation: Sister

Name   : Beth   Owner: Sparks, R.
Date   : 1814/04/06   Page : 051
Bequeath: Sparks, Ruth
Relation: Wife

Name   : Betsy   Owner: Brisco, Thomas
Date   : 1832/04/18   Page : 232
Bequeath: Brisco, Twilland
Relation: Son

NAMES FROM WILLBOOK

Name   : Betsy   Owner: Durbin, Daniel
Date   : 1822/03/05   Page : 200
Bequeath: Durbin, Elizabeth
Relation: Wife

Name   : Betsy   Owner: Hannah, James
Date   : 1826/07/11   Page : 160
Bequeath: Robinson, Ann
Relation: Daughter

Name   : Betta   Owner: Brashears,
                                 Turner
Date   : 1817/11/24   Page : 079
Bequeath: Gibson, Rebecca
Relation: Daughter
Children: Jefferson

Name   : Betty   Owner: Brashears,
                                 Turner
Date   : 1833/05/30   Page : 276
Bequeath: Brashears, Amelia
Relation: Daughter

Name   : Betty   Owner: Crane, Waterman
Date   : 1829/02/05   Page : 149
Bequeath: Christie, Caroline
Relation: Grandaughter

Name   : Bill   Owner: Brashears,
                                 Marsham
Date   : 1831/01/17
Page   : 230
Bequeath: Brashears, Turner
Relation: Son

Name   : Bill   Owner: Freeland,
                                 Frisby
Date   : 1817/??/??
Page   : 081
Bequeath: Freeland, Augustus
Relation: Son

Name   : Bill   Owner: Gibson, Samual
Date   : 1817/11/24   Page : 079

NAMES FROM WILLBOOK

Bill(cont)
Bequeath: Gibson, Joshua
Relation: Son
Parents : Vincent and Nedi.
Siblings: Burr, Lee and Jeremy.

Name   : Bill   Owner: Robinson, Seth
Date   : 1810/06/05   Page : 054
Note   : Bill was to be sold.

Name   : Billy   Owner: Bassett,
                                  William
Date   : 1820/05/24   Page : 128
Bequeath: Davis, Betsy
Relation: Cousin

Name   : Billy   Owner: Brashears,
                                  Turner
Date   : 1833/05/30   Page : 276
Bequeath: Brashears, Joseph
Relation: Son

Name   : Billy   Owner: Bullock, Mary
Date   : 1833/05/17   Page : 273
Wife   : Patty
Children: Jim, Flora, Alexander, Tenach, Rhoda,
          New, Vira, Melinda and Sarah.
Note: Billy was emancipated and sent to
Liberia, along with his wife and children.

Name   : Boatswain   Owner: Gibson, Samual
Date   : 1817/11/24   Page : 079
Bequeath: Gibson, Rebecca
Relation: Daughter

Name   : Bob   Owner: Barnes, Esther
Date   : 1831/10/05   Page : 288
Bequeath: Barnes, Elias
Relation: Son

Name   : Bob   Owner: Barnes, Thomas
Date   : 1817/03/17   Page : 071
Bequeath: Barnes, Thomas
Relation: Wife

NAMES FROM WILLBOOK

Name   : Bob   Owner: Watts, Nancy
Date   : 1831/04/12   Page : 226
Note: Bob was emmancipated by his grandmother
Nancy Watts (a free woman of color).

Name   : Brewer   Owner: Gibson, Tobias
Date   : 1804/10/26   Page : 218
Bequeath: Watkins, Lary
Relation: Daughter

Name   : Albert   Owner: Green, Abram
Date   : 1826/06/06   Page : 011
Note   : Emancipated.

Name   : Buck   Owner: Brisco, Thomas
Date   : 1830/04/18   Page : 232
Bequeath: Brisco, Claiborne
Relation: Son

Name   : Burr   Owner: Gibson, Samual
Date   : 1817/11/24   Page : 079
Bequeath: Gibson, Joshua
Relation: Son
Parents : Vincent and Nedi.
Siblings: Bill, Lee and Jeremy.

Name   : Caleb   Owner: Brashears,
                                   Turner
Date   : 1833/05/30   Page : 276
Bequeath: Brashears,Joseph
Relation: Son

Name   : Casey   Owner: Freeland,
                                   Frisby
Date   : 1817/??/??   Page : 081
Bequeath: Freeland,Augustus
Relation: Son

Name   : Carigo?   Owner: Brashears,
                                   Martha
Date   : 1814/04/16   Page : 051
Bequeath: Brashears, Turner
Relation: Son

NAMES FROM WILLBOOK

Name   : Caroline   Owner: Brashears,
                                      Turner
Date   : 1833/05/30   Page : 276
Bequeath: Brashears, Joseph
Relation: Son

Name   : Caroline   Owner: Durbin, Daniel
Date   : 1822/03/05   Page : 200
Bequeath: Durbin, Elizabeth
Relation: Wife

Name   : Cassandra   Owner: Durbin, Daniel
Date   : 1822/03/05   Page : 200
Bequeath: Durbin, Elizabeth
Relation: Wife

Name   : Cato   Owner: Cobun, Samuel
Date   : 1813/05/10   Page : 042
Bequeath: Cobun, Samuel
          Cobun, John
Relation: Sons

Name   : Caty   Owner: Barnes, Joseph
Date   : 1821/04/08   Page : 134
Bequeath: Barnes, Harriet
Relation: Sister?

Name   : Celia   Owner: Stampley, Jacob
Date   : 1829/06/02   Page : 162
Bequeath: Stampley, Mary U.
Relation: Daughter

Name   : Chan   Owner: Bassett,
                                      William
Date   : 1820/05/24   Page : 128
Bequeath: Davis, Betsy
Relation: Cousin

Name   : Chana   Owner: Clark, Gibson
Date   : 1820/01/23   Page : 088
Note: Chana was bequeathed to the children of
Elijah Clark's son.

Name   : Chana   Owner: Gibson, James

8

NAMES FROM WILLBOOK

Chana (cont)
Date   : 1822/10/03   Page : 136
Bequeath: Gibson, Elizabeth
Relation: Wife
Note: Chana was about 22. She was to remain with Elizabeth for ten years and then become the property of Teresa Caroline McGirty, neice of Elizabeth.

Name   : Charles   Owner: Brashears, Marsham
Date   : 1831/01/17   Page : 230
Bequeath: Brashears, Turner
Relation: Son
Note: Charles was called "Big" Charles.

Name   : Charles   Owner: Brisco, Thomas
Date   : 1832/04/18   Page : 232
Bequeath: Brisco, Claiborne
Relation: Son

Name   : Charles   Owner: Clark, Gibson
Date   : 1820/01/23   Page : 088
Bequeath: Heddrick
Note: Charles was bequeathed to the children of Gibson Clark's deceased daughter, Nancy Heddrick.

Name   : Charles   Owner: Crane, Waterman
Date   : 1829/02/05   Page : 149
Bequeath: Crane, Catherine
Relation: Wife
Parents : Isaac and Mill.
Siblings: May, Joe and Ann.

Name   : Charles   Owner: Green, Abram
Date   : 1826/06/02   Page : 168
Bequeath: unborn infant

Name   : Charles   Owner: Moors, Robert
Date   : 1817/02/18   Page : 076
Bequeath: Robert Moor's Fiance.

Name   : Charles

NAMES FROM WILLBOOK

Charles(cont)

```
                              Owner: Phillips,
                                     Jenken
Date      : 1819/11/29   Page : 212
Bequeath: Elenor Hamilton's surving Child.
Relation: ?
```

```
Name      : Charles       Owner: Stampley, Jacob
Date      : 1829/06/02    Page : 162
Bequeath: Stampley, David
          Stampley, Samuel
Relation: Sons
Mother   : Sarah
Siblings: Letty, Charlotte and Susey.
```

```
Name      : Charlotte     Owner: Brisco, Thomas
Date      : 1830/04/18    Page : 232
Bequeath: Brisco, Virly
Relation: Wife
Husband  : Perry
```

```
Name      : Charlotte     Owner: Brokus,
                                 Charolotte
Date      : 1805/10/05    Page : 016
Bequeath: Brokus, Ann
Relation: Wife
```

```
Name      : Charlotte     Owner: Bullock, Mary
Date      : 1833/05/17    Page : 273
Note: Emancipated.
```

```
Name      : Charlotte     Owner: Durbin, Daniel
Date      : 1822/03/05    Page : 200
Bequeath: Phillips, Gabriel
          Phillips, Sarah
Relation: ?
Note: Charlotte's children were also
bequeathed to the Phillips.
```

```
Name      : Charlotte     Owner: Clabon, Harris
Date      : 1821/08/24    Page : 124
Bequeath: Clabon, Melvina
Relation: Daughter
```

NAMES FROM WILLBOOK

```
Name      : Charlotte         Owner: Stampley, Jacob
Date      : 1829/06/02        Page : 162
Bequeath  : Stampley, David
            Stampley, Samual
Relation  : Sons
Mother    : Sarah
Siblings  : Letty, Charles and Susey.

Name      : Clara             Owner: Barnes, Esther
Date      : 1831/10/05        Page : 288
Bequeath  : Barnes, Hariett
Relation  : Daughter
Note: Clara's children were also bequeathed to
Hariett Barnes.

Name      : Clarkey?          Owner: Moors, Robert
Date      : 1817/02/18        Page : 076
Bequeath  : Moors, Johil?
Relation  : Son

Name      : Clarisa           Owner: Brashears,
                                     Robert
Date      : 1833/05/30        Page : 276
Bequeath  : Brashears, Amelia
Relation  : Daughter

Note      : Cloe              Owner: Barnes, Esther
Date      : 1814/04/16        Page : 051
Bequeath  : Brashears, Prisilla
Relation  : Daughter
Children  : Silva and Daphney.

Name      : Diley             Owner: Moors, Robert
Date      : 1817/02/18        Page :076
Relation  : Robert Moor's     Fiance.

Name      : Dina              Owner: Crane, Waterman
Date      : 1829/02/05        Page : 149
Bequeath  : Watson, James M.
Relation  : Grandson
Children  : Hary, Grace, Dan, Tora, Dick,
            Patience and Moses.
Note      : William Young, (son-in-law of
Waterman Crane) was the Trustee for James.
```

NAMES FROM WILLBOOK

Name   : Dinah   Owner: Clabon, Harris
Date   : 1821/08/24   Page : 124
Bequeath: Clabon, Melvina
Relation: Daughter

Name   : Dinah   Owner: Stampley, Jacob
Date   : 1829/06/02   Page : 162
Bequeath: Stampley, Nancy C.
Relation: Daughter

Name   : Doil?   Owner: Freeland,
                                    Frisby
Date   : 1817/01/01   Page : 081
Bequeath: Freeland, Thomas
Relation: Son

Name   : Doll   Owner: Gibson, Tobias
Date   : 1804/10/06   Page : 011
Husband : Jo
Note: Doll was to be emancipated four years after Tobias's death.

Name   : Dolly   Owner: Brisco, Thomas
Date   : 1832/04/18   Page : 232
Bequeath: Brisco, Claiborne
Relation: Son

Name   : Dorcus   Owner: Clabon, Harris
Date   : 1821/08/24   Page : 124
Bequeath: Clabon, Melvina
Relation: Daughter

Name   : Doze   Owner: Crane, Waterman
Date   : 1829/02/05   Page : 149
Bequeath: Watson, James M.
Relation: Grandson
Mother : Hen
Note: William Young, (son-in-law of Waterman Crane) was the Trustee for James M. Watson.

Name   : Eliza   Owner: Brashears,
                                    Turner
Date   : 1833/05/30   Page : 276
Bequeath: Brashears, Amelia

NAMES FROM WILLBOOK

Eliza(cont)
Relation: Daughter

Name   : Eliza   Owner: Brashears,
                                      Marsham
Date   : 1831/01/17   Page : 230
Bequeath: Brashears, Turner
Relation: Son

Name   : Eliza   Owner: Crane, Waterman
Date   : 1829/02/05   Page : 149
Bequeath: Crane, Catherine
Relation: Wife
Parents : Prince and Sue.
Siblings: John, Jacob and Lina.

Name   : Eliza   Owner: Durbin, Daniel
Date   : 1822/03/05   Page : 200
Bequeath: Durbin, Elizabeth
Relation: Wife

Name   : Eliza   Owner: Clabon, Harris
Date   : 1821/08/24   Page : 124
Bequeath: Clabon, Melvina
Relation: Daughter

Name   : Elly   Owner: Brashears,
                                      Marsham
Date   : 1831/01/17   Page : 230
Bequeath: Brashears, Turner
Relation: Son

Name   : Elsey   Owner: Daniel, Ann
Date   : 1830/07/26   Page : 218
Bequeath: Taylor, Mary
Relation: Daughter

Name   : Emily   Owner: Brashears,
                                      Turner
Date   : 1833/05/30   Page : 276
Bequeath: Brashears, Amelia
Relation: Daughter

Name   : Emily   Owner: McCaleb, William

NAMES FROM WILLBOOK

Emily (cont)
Date   : 1813/08/09   Page : 049
Bequeath: McCaleb, Ann
Relation: Wife
Mother   : Sally

Name   : Eose?   Owner: Foster, William
Date   : 1812/02/10   Page : 038
Bequeath: Tbeatha, Eliza
Relation: Daughter

Name   : Ephram   Owner: Barnes, Esther
Date   : 1831/10/05   Page : 288
Bequeath: Barnes, Esther
Relation: Son

Name   : Esther   Owner: Clark, Gibson
Date   : 1820/01/23   Page : 088
Note: Esther was bequeathed to the children of son Elijah Clark.

Name   : Esther   Owner: Crane, Waterman
Date   : 1829/02/05   Page : 149
Bequeath: James M. Watson
Relation: Grandson
Note: William Young, (son-in-law of Waterman Crane) was the Trustee for James M. Watson. Esther was William's Nurse.

Name   : Esther   Owner: Foster, William
Date   : 1812/02/10   Page : 038
Bequeath: Smith, Sally
Relation: Daughter

Name   : Evaline   Owner: Green, Abram
Date   : 1826/06/02   Page : 168
Bequeath: Green, Andrew
Relation: Son
Husband : Tarleton
Note: Andrew Green was also bequeathed the children of Eveline and Tarleton.

Name   : Fanny   Owner: Freeland, Frisby

NAMES FROM WILLBOOK

Fanny(cont)
Date   : 1817/01/01   Page : 081
Bequeath: Freeland, Thomas
Relation: Son

Name   : Fanny   Owner: Clabon, Harris
Date   : 1821/08/24   Page : 124
Bequeath: Clabon, Henderson
Relation: Son

Name   : Fanny?   Owner: McCaleb, William
Date   : 1813/08/09   Page : 049
Bequeath: McCaleb, Jane
Relation: Daughter
Note: Fanny's name may have also been Fancy.

Name   : Ferndall   Owner: Foster, William
Date   : 1812/02/10   Page : 038
Bequeath: Foster, Rebeckah
Relation: Daughter

Name   : Flora   Owner: Bullock, Mary
Date   : 1833/05/17   Page : 273
Parents   : Billy and Patty.
Siblings: Jim, Alexander, Tenach, Rhoda, New, Vira and Melinda.
Note: Flora was emancipated and sent to Libera with her parents and siblings.

Name   : Florence   Owner: Green, Abram
Date   : 1826/06/02   Page : 168
Bequeath: Green, Andrew
Relation: Son

Name   : Fortune   Owner: Brokus, William
Date   : 1805/10/06   Page : 016
Bequeath: Brokus, Ann
Relation: Wife

Name   : Frank   Owner: Barnes, Esther
Date   : 1831/10/05   Page : 288
Bequeath: Barnes, Elias
Relation: Son

NAMES FROM WILLBOOK

Name   : Frank   Owner: Clabon, Harris
Date   : 1821/08/24   Page : 124
Bequeath: Clabon, Melvina
Relation: Daughter

Name   : Gearl   Owner: Moors, Robert
Date   : 1817/02/18   Page : 076
Bequeath: Robert Moor's Fiance.

Name   : George   Owner: Green, Abram
Date   : 1826/06/02   Page : 168
Bequeath: Green, Ann
Relation: Wife

Name   : George   Owner: Saxon, Joshua
Date   : 1817/01/31   Page : 063
Bequeath: Saxon, Medar
Relation: Wife

Name   : George   Owner: Thompson, John
Date   : 1833/03/30   Page : 290
Note   : George was to remain on John Thompson's farm.

Name   : Grace   Owner: Crane, Waterman
Date   : 1829/02/05   Page : 149
Bequeath: Watson, James M.
Relation: Grandson
Mother   : Dina
Siblings : Hary, Dan, Tora, Dick, Patience and Moses.
Note: William Young (Son-in-law of Waterman Crane) was the Truestee for James M. Watson.

Name   : Hannah   Owner: Green, Abram
Date   : 1826/06/02   Page : 168
Bequeath: Green, Martha
Relation: Daughter

Name   : Harriet   Owner: Brashears, Turner
Date   : 1833/05/30   Page : 276
Bequeath: Brashears, Amelia
Relation: Daughter

NAMES FROM WILLBOOK

Name   : Harriet   Owner: Brashears,
                                      Marsham
Date   : 1831/01/17   Page :230
Bequeath: Brashears, Turner
Relation: Son

Name   : Harriet   Owner: Durbin, Daniel
Date   : 1822/03/05   Page : 200
Bequeath: Durbin, Elizabeth
Relation: Wife

Name   : Harrison   Owner: Brashears,
                                      Turner
Date   : 1833/05/30   Page : 276
Bequeath: Brashears, Joseph
Relation: Son

Name   : Harry   Owner: Cobun, Samuel
Date   : 1813/05/10   Page : 042
Bequeath: Cobun, Samuel
           Cobun, John
Relation: Sons

Name   : Harry   Owner: Daniel, Ann
Date   : 1830/07/26   Page : 218
Bequeath: Daniel, William
Relation: Son

Name   : Harvey   Owner: Saxon, Joshua
Date   : 1817/01/31   Page : 063
Bequeath: Saxon, Samual
Relation: Son

Name   : Hary   Owner: Crane, Waterman
Date   : 1829/02/05   Page : 149
Bequeath: Watson, James M.
Relation: Grandson
Mother   : Dina
Siblings: Grace, Dan, Tora, Dick, Patience and
           Moses.
Note: William Young (son-in-law of Waterman
Crane was trustee for James M. Watson.

Name   : Hay   Owner: Saxon, Joshua

17

NAMES FROM WILLBOOK

Hay(cont)
Date   : 1817/01/31   Page : 063
Bequeath: Saxon, Medar
Relation: Wife

Name   : Hen   Owner: Crane, Waterman
Date   : 1829/02/05   Page : 149
Bequeath: Watson, James M.
Relation: Grandson
Child   : Doze
Note: William Young (son-in-law of Waterman Crane) was trustee for James M. Watson.

Name   : Henry   Owner: Brisco, Thomas
Date   : 1832/04/18   Page : 232
Bequeath: Brisco, Twilland
Relation: Son

Name   : Henry   Owner: Crane, Waterman
Date   : 1829/02/05   Page : 149
Bequeath: McNeil, James
Relation: Grandson

Name   : Henry   Owner: Freeland,
                                 Frisby
Date   : 1817/??/??   Page : 081
Bequeath: Freeland, Thomas
Relation: Son

Name   : Henry   Owner: Thompson, John
Date   : 1833/03/30   Page : 290
Note   : Henry was to remain on John Thompson's Farm.

Name   : Isaac   Owner: Barnes, Esther
Date   : 1831/10/05   Page : 288
Bequeath: Barnes, Elias
Relation: Son

Name   : Isaac   Owner: Crane, Waterman
Date   : 1829/02/05   Page : 149
Bequeath: Crane, Catherine
Relation: Wife

18

NAMES FROM WILLBOOK

Name   : Isaac   Owner: Crane, Waterman
Date   : 1829/02/05   Page : 149
Bequeath: Crane, James
Relation: Son

Name   : Isaac   Owner: Moors, Robert
Date   : 1817/02/18   Page : 076
Bequeath: Moors, James
Relation: Son

Name   : Isam   Owner: Gibson, James
Date   : 1822/10/03   Page : 136
Bequeath: Gibson, Elizabeth
Relation: Wife
Note: Isam was about thirty-five years old.

Name   : Isam   Owner: Thompson, John
Date   : 1833/03/30   Page : 290
Note: Isam was to remain on John Thompson's farm.

Name   : Jack   Owner: Barnes, Esther
Date   : 1831/10/05   Page : 288
Bequeath: Barnes, Elias
Relation: Son

Name   : Jack   Owner: Durbin, Daniel
Date   : 1822/03/05   Page : 200
Bequeath: Durbin, Elizabeth
Relation: Wife

Name   : Jack   Owner: Clabon, Harris
Date   : 1821/08/24   Page : 124
Bequeath: Clabon, Henderson
Relation: Son

Name   : Jack   Owner: Robinson, Seth
Date   : 1810/06/05   Page : 054
Note: Jack was to be sold.

Name   : Jack   Owner: Stampley, Jacob
Date   : 1829/06/02   Page : 162
Bequeath: Stampley, James
Relation: Son

NAMES FROM WILLBOOK

Name   : Jack   Owner: Thompson, John
Date   : 1833/03/30   Page : 290
Note: Jack was to remain on John Thompson's farm.

Name   : Jacob   Owner: Brashears, Martha
Date   : 1814/04/16   Page : 051
Bequeath: Brashears, Tobias
Relation: Son

Name   : Jacob   Owner: Cafferg, Mary
Date   : 1819/06/20   Page : 143
Bequeath: Cafferg, Jefferson
Relation: Son

Name   : Jacob   Owner: Clark, Gibson
Date   : 1820/01/23   Page : 088
Bequeath: Clark, Susanah
Relation: Grandaughter

Name   : Jacob   Owner: Crane, Waterman
Date   : 1829/02/05   Page : 149
Bequeath: Crane, Catherine
Relation: Wife
Parents : Prince and Sue.
Siblings: John, Lina and Eliza.

Name   : Jacob   Owner: Freeland, Frisby
Date   : 1817/??/??   Page : 081
Bequeath: Freeland, Thomas
Relation: Son

Name   : Jacob   Owner: Hanna, James
Date   : 1826/07/11   Page : 160
Bequeath: Hanna, William
Relation: Brother

Name   : James   Owner: Brashears, Martha
Date   : 1814/04/16   Page : 051
Bequeath: Brashears, Tobias
Relation: Son

NAMES FROM WILLBOOK

Name   : James   Owner: Brashears,
                                     Turner
Date   : 1833/05/30   Page : 276
Bequeath: Brashears, Joseph
Relation: Son

Name   : James   Owner: Phillips,
                                     Jenkins
Date   : 1819/11/29   Page : 212
Bequeath: Jenkins, Phillips
Relation: Grandson?

Name   : James   Owner: Saxon, Joshua
Date   : 1817/01/31   Page : 063
Bequeath: Saxon, Medar
Relation: Wife
Wife   : Hay

Name   : Jane   Owner: Brashears, Jane
Date   : 1831/01/17   Page : 230
Bequeath: Turner, Brashears
Relation: ?

Name   : Jane   Owner: Freeland,
                                     Frisby
Date   : 1817/??/??   Page : 081
Bequeath: Freeland, Thomas
Relation: Son

Name   : Jane   Owner: Saxon, Joshua
Date   : 1817/01/31   Page : 063
Bequeath: Ingram, Charlotte
Relation: Daughter

Name   : January   Owner: Robinson, John
Date   : 1830/??/??   Page : 223
Bequeath: Robinson, Nancy
Relation: Wife

Name   : Jefferson   Owner: Gibson, Samual
Date   : 1817/11/24   Page : 079
Bequeath: Gibson, Rebecca
Relation: Daughter
Mother   : Betta

NAMES FROM WILLBOOK

Name   : Jesse   Owner: Barnes, Abram
Date   : 1830/01/25   Page : 224
Bequeath: Leyborne, Mary?

Name   : Jenney   Owner: Moors, Robert
Date   : 1817/02/18   Page : 076
Bequeath: Moors, Elizabeth
Relation: Daughter

Name   : Jenny   Owner: Barnes, Esther
Date   : 1831/10/05   Page : 288
Bequeath: Barnes, Elias
Relation: Daughter

Name   : Jeremy   Owner: Gibson, Samual
Date   : 1817/11/24   Page : 079
Bequeath: Gibson, Joshua
Relation: Son
Parents : Vincent and Nedi
Siblings : Bill, Burr and Lee.

Name   : Jim   Owner: Basset, William
Date   : 1820/05/24   Page : 128
Bequeath: Davis, Sarah
Relation: Daughter

Name   : Jim   Owner: Brashears, Turner
Date   : 1833/05/30   Page : 276
Bequeath: Brashears, Amelia
Relation: Daughter

Name   : Jim   Owner: Bullock, Mary
Date   : 1833/05/17   Page : 273
Parents : Billy and Patty.
Siblings : Flora, Alexander, Tenach, Rhoda, New, Vira, Melinda and Sarah.
Note: Jim was emancipated and sent to Liberia with his parents and siblings.

Name   : Jim   Owner: Clark, Gibson
Date   : 1820/01/23   Page : 088
Note: Jim was bequeathed to the children of Gibson Clark son Elijah Clark.

NAMES FROM WILLBOOK

Name   : Jim   Owner: Crane, Waterman
Date   : 1829/02/05   Page : 149
Bequeath: Crane, James
Relation: Son

Name   : Jim   Owner: Crane, Waterman
Date   : 1829/02/05   Page : 149
Bequeath: McNeil, Robert
Relation: Grandson
Note: Jim was called "Yellow" Jim.

Name   : Jim   Owner: Clabon, Harris
Date   : 1821/08/24   Page : 124
Bequeath: Clabon, Henderson
Relation: Son

Name   : Jim   Owner: Stampley, Jacob
Date   : 1829/06/02   Page : 162
Bequeath: Stampley, David
          Stampley, Samual
Relation: Son

Name   : Jo   Owner: Gibson, Tobias
Date   : 1804/10/02   Page : 162
Wife   : Doll
Note: Jo was emancipated.

Name   : Jack   Owner: Thompson, John
Date   : 1833/03/06   Page : 011
Wife   : Doll
Note: Jack was to be emancipated four years after John Thompson's death.

Name   : Joe   Owner: Crane, Waterman
Date   : 1829/02/05   Page : 149
Bequeath: Crane, Catherine
Relation: Wife
Parents : Isaac and Mill.
Siblings: Charles, Mary and Ann.

Name   : Joe   Owner: Wooldrige, W. H.
Date   : 1810/04/18   Page :053
Bequeath: Wooldridge, Elam
Relation: Son

NAMES FROM WILLBOOK

Name   : John   Owner: Crane, Waterman
Date   : 1829/02/05   Page : 149
Bequeath: Crane, Elizabeth
Relation: Wife
Parents : Prince and Sue.
Siblings: Jacob, Lina and Eliza.

Name   : John   Owner: Waterman, Crane
Date   : 1829/02/05   Page :149
Bequeath: Young, Clarissa
Relation: Daughter

Name   : John   Owner: Freeland,
                                    Frisby
Date   : 1817/01/01   Page : 081
Bequeath: Freeland, John
Relation: Son

Name   : John   Owner: Hanna, James
Date   : 1826/07/11   Page : 160
Bequeath: Hanna, William
Relation: Brother

Name   : John Prince   Owner: Crane, Waterman
Date   : 1829/02/05   Page : 149
Bequeath: McNeil, Robert
Relation: Grandson

Name   : Joseph   Owner: Brisco, Thomas
Date   : 1832/04/18   Page : 232
Bequeath: Brisco, Claiborne
Relation: Son

Name   : Joshua   Owner: Freeland,
                                    Frisby
Date   : 1817/??/??   Page : 081
Bequeath: Freeland, Thomas
Relation: Son

Name   : Judah   Owner: Durbin, Daniel
Date   : 1822/03/05   Page : 200
Bequeath: Durbin, Elizabeth
Relation: Wife

NAMES FROM WILLBOOK

Name   : Julia   Owner: Brashears,
                                  Martha
Date   : 1814/04/16   Page : 051
Bequeath: Brashears, Marsham
Relation: Son

Name   : Julia   Owner: Brashears,
                                  Turner
Date   : 1833/05/30   Page : 276
Bequeath: Brashears, Amelia
Relation: Daughter

Name   : Kesiah   Owner: Clabon, Harris
Date   : 1821/08/24   Page : 124
Bequeath: Clabon, Henderson
Relation: Son

Name   : Kitty   Owner: Phillips,
                                  Jenken
Date   : 1819/11/29   Page : 212
Note: Kitty was bequeathed to Elenor
Hamilton's surving child.

Name   : Lander   Owner: Brashears,
                                  Martha
Date   : 1814/04/16   Page : 051
Bequeath: Brashears, Marsham
Relation: Son

Name   : Laney   Owner: Clabon, Harris
Date   : 1821/08/24   Page : 124
Bequeath: Clabon, Melvina
Relation: Daughter

Name   : Lauder   Owner: Brashears,
                                  Marsham
Date   : 1831/01/17   Page : 230
Bequeath: Brashears, Turner
Relation: Son

Name   : Laura   Owner: Hanna, James
Date   : 1826/07/11   Page : 160
Bequeath: Dreaer, Jane
Relation: Son

NAMES FROM WILLBOOK

Name   : Leander   Owner: Green, Abram
Date   : 1826/06/02   Page : 168
Bequeath: Green, Ann
Relation: Wife

Name   : Lee   Owner: Gibson, Samual
Date   : 1817/11/24   Page : 079
Bequeath: Gibson, Joshua
Relation: Son
Parents : Vincent and Nedi.
Siblings: Bill, Burr and Jeremy.

Name   : Leogis?   Owner: Freeland,
                                     Frisby
Date   : 1817/??/??   Page : 081
Bequeath: Freeland, Thomas
Relation: Son

Name   : Letty   Owner: Stampley,
                                     Jacob
Date   : 1829/06/02   Page : 162
Bequeath: Stampley, David
          Stampley, Samual
Relation: Sons
Mother : Sarah
Siblings: Charlotte, Charles and Susey.

Name   : Levi   Owner: Brashears,
                                     Turner
Date   : 1833/05/30   Page : 276
Bequeath: Brashears, Joseph
Relation: Son

Name   : Leving   Owner: Hanna, James
Date   : 1826/07/11   Page : 160
Bequeath: Robinson, Ann
Relation: Son

Name   : Lewis   Owner: Robinson, John
Date   : 1830/??/??   Page : 223
Bequeath: Robinson, Nancy
Relation: Wife

Name   : Lickey

NAMES FROM WILLBOOK

Lickey(cont)
                              Owner: Brashears,
                                     Marsham
Date   : 1831/01/17   Page : 230
Bequeath: Brashears, Turner
Relation: Son

Name   : Lina   Owner: Crane,
                                     Waterman
Date   : 1829/02/05   Page : 149
Bequeath: Crane, Waterman
Relation: Wife
Parents : Prince and Sue.
Siblings: John, Jacob and Eliza.

Name   : Linda   Owner: Foster,
                                     William
Date   : 1812/02/10   Page : 038
Bequeath: Foster, Rebeckah
Relation: Daughter

Name   : Linda   Owner: Stampley,
                                     Jacob
Date   : 1829/06/02   Page : 162
Bequeath: Stampley, Sarah
Relation: Daughter
Child   : Sarah

Name   : Linny   Owner: Hanna, James
Date   : 1826/07/11   Page : 160
Bequeath: Robinson, Ann
Relation: Son

Name   : Liza   Owner: Prescott, Abel
Date   : 1833/05/26   Page : 268
Relation: ?
Child   : Tom

Name   : Louis   Owner: Green, Abram
Date   : 1826/06/02   Page : 168
Bequeath: Green, Ann
Relation: Wife

Name   : Louisa   Owner: Brisco, Thomas

NAMES FROM WILLBOOK

Louisa (cont)
Date   : 1832/04/18   Page : 232
Bequeath: Brisco, Twilland
Relation: Son

Name   : Lucinda   Owner: Cafferg, Mary
Date   : 1819/06/20   Page : 143
Bequeath: Cafferg, Jefferson
Relation: Son

Name   : Lucinda   Owner: Crane, Waterman
Date   : 1829/02/05   Page : 149
Bequeath: Quinn, Catherine
Relation: ?
Child   : Solomon

Name   : Lucinda   Owner: Thompson, John
Date   : 1833/03/30   Page : 290
Note: Lucinda was to remain on John Thompson's farm.

Name   : Lucy   Owner: Clarke, Lewis
Date   : 1825/10/30   Page : 206
Bequeath: Brinton, Piety
Relation: Grandaughter

Name   : Lucy   Owner: Green, Abram
Date   : 1826/06/02   Page : 168
Bequeath: Infant
Relation: Son

Name   : Lucy   Owner: Stampley, Jacob
Date   : 1829/06/02   Page : 162
Bequeath: Stampley, Mary U.
Relation: Daughter

Name   : Lunia   Owner: Jenken, Phillips
Date   : 1819/11/29   Page : 212
Note: Lunia was bequeated to Elenor Hamilton's surviving child.

NAMES FROM WILLBOOK

Name   : Lyle   Owner: Sparks, R.
Date   : 1814/04/06   Page : 051
Bequeath: Sparks, Ruth
Relation: Wife

Name   : Major   Owner: Barnes, Joseph
Date   : 1821/04/08   Page : 134
Bequeath: Barnes, Harriet
Relation: Sister?

Name   : Malinda   Owner: Green, Abram
Date   : 1826/06/02   Page : 168
Bequeath: Infant

Name   : Manson   Owner: Brashears,
                                    Turner
Date   : 1833/05/30   Page : 276
Bequeath: Brashears, Amelia
Relation: Daughter

Name   : Manuel   Owner: Barnes, Esther
Date   : 1831/10/05   Page : 288
Bequeath: Barnes, Elias
Relation: Son

Name   : March   Owner: Green, Abram
Date   : 1826/06/02   Page : 165
Bequeath: Green, Andrew
Relation: Son

Name   : Maria   Owner: Barnes, Abram
Date   : 1830/01/25   Page : 224
Bequeath: Leyborne, Mary
Relation: ?

Name   : Maria   Owner: Thompson, John
Date   : 1833/03/30   Page : 290
Note: Maria was to remain on John Thompson's farm.

Name   : Maria   Owner: Brashears,
                                    Martha
Date   : 1814/04/16   Page : 051
Bequeath: Brashears, Tobias

NAMES FROM WILLBOOK

Maria (cont)
Relation: Son

Name   : Mariah   Owner: Crane,
                                   Waterman
Date   : 1829/02/05   Page : 149
Bequeath: Christie, Caroline
Relation: Grandaughter
Parents : Tan and Robin.
Sibling : Washington

Name   : Mariah   Owner: Green, Abram
Date   : 1826/06/02   Page : 168
Bequeath: Green, Martha
Relation: Daughter

Name   : Mariah   Owner: Clabon, Harris
Date   : 1821/08/24   Page : 124
Bequeath: Clabon, Henderson
Relation: Son

Name   : Mark   Owner: Durbin, Daniel
Date   : 1822/03/05   Page : 200
Bequeath: Durbin, Elizabeth
Relation: Wife

Name   : Martha   Owner: Brashears,
                                   Turner
Date   : 1833/05/30   Page : 276
Bequeath: Brashears, Amelia
Relation: Daughter

Name   : Mary   Owner: Bassett,
                                   William
Date   : 1820/05/24   Page : 128
Bequeath: Bassett, Huston
Relation: Brother

Name   : Mary   Owner: Brashears,
                                   Turner
Date   : 1833/05/30   Page : 276
Bequeath: Brashears, Catherine
Relation: Wife

NAMES FROM WILLBOOK

Name   : Mary   Owner: Brokus,
                                      William
Date   : 1805/10/05   Page : 016
Bequeath: Brokus, Ann
Relation: Wife

Name   : Mary   Owner: Crane,
                                      Waterman
Date   : 1829/02/05   Page : 149
Bequeath: Crane, Catherine
Relation: Wife
Parents : Isaac and Mill.
Siblings: Charles, Joe and Ann.

Name   : Mary   Owner: Crane,
                                      Waterman
Date   : 1829/02/05   Page : 149
Bequeath: Crane,Catherine
Relation: Wife

Name   : Mary   Owner: Clabon, Harris
Date   : 1821/08/24   Page : 124
Bequeath: Clabon, Henderson
Relation: Son

Name   : Mary   Owner: Wooldridge,
                                      W.H.
Date   : 1810/04/18   Page : 053
Bequeath: Wooldridge, Elam
Relation: Son

Name   : Mary Ann   Owner: Breazeale,
                                      Willis
Date   : 1833/05/30   Page : 234
Bequeath: Allen, Dan
Relation: ?
Child   : Dan Allen

Name   : Matilda   Owner: Phillips,
                                      Jenken
Date   : 1819/11/29   Page : 212
Bequeath: Hamilton, Lucy
Relation: Grandaughter

NAMES FROM WILLBOOK

Name   : May   Owner: Durbin, Daniel
Date   : 1822/03/05   Page : 200
Bequeath: Durbin, Elizabeth
Relation: Grandaughter

Name   : Melinda   Owner: Bullock, Mary
Date   : 1833/05/17   Page : 273
Parents : Billy and Patty.
Siblings: Jim, Flora, Alexander, Tenach, Rhoda,
          New and Vira.
Note: Melinda was emancipated and sent to
Liberia with her parents and siblings.

Name   : Milanda   Owner: Brisco, Thomas
Date   : 1832/04/18   Page : 232
Bequeath: Brisco, Twilland
Relation: Son

Name   : Mill   Owner: Crane,
                                    Waterman
Date   : 1829/02/05   Page : 149
Bequeath: Crane, Catherine
Relation: Wife
Husband : Isaac
Children: Charles, Mary, Joe and Ann.

Name   : Milly   Owner: Stampley,
                                    Jacob
Date   : 1829/06/02   Page : 162
Bequeath: Black, Napoleon
Relation: Son

Name   : Mima   Owner: Green, Ann
Date   : 1826/06/02   Page : 168
Bequeath: Green, Ann
Relation: Wife

Name   : Minda   Owner: Green, Abram
Date   : 1826/06/02   Page : 168
Bequeath: Green, Andrew
Relation: Son

Name   : Mingo   Owner: Gibson, Tobias
Date   : 1804/10/06   Page : 011

NAMES FROM WILLBOOK

Mingo(cont)
Note: Mingo was Emancipated.

Name   : Misty   Owner: Barnes,
                                     Esther
Date   : 1831/10/06   Page : 288
Bequeath: Barnes, Elias
Relation: Son

Name   : Mitton   Owner: Thompson, John
Date   : 1833/03/30   Page : 290
Note: Mitton was to remain on John Thompson's farm.

Name   : Moracia   Owner: Durbin, Daniel
Date   : 1822/03/05   Page : 200
Bequeath: Durbin, Elizabeth
Relation: Wife

Name   : Morgan   Owner: Brisco, Thomas
Date   : 1832/04/18   Page : 232
Bequeath: Brisco, Twilland
Relation: Son

Name   : Moses   Owner: Brashears,
                                     Marsham
Date   : 1831/01/17   Page : 230
Bequeath: Brashears, Turner
Relation: Son

Name   : Moses   Owner: Brisco, Thomas
Date   : 1832/04/18   Page : 232
Bequeath: Brisco, ?
Relation: Son

Name   : Moses   Owner: Crane,
                                     Waterman
Date   : 1829/02/05   Page : 149
Bequeath: Watson, James M.
Relation: Grandson
Mother : Dina
Siblings: Hary, Grace, Dan, Tora, Dick and
          Patience.

NAMES FROM WILLBOOK

Moses(cont)
Note: William Young (son-in-law of Waterman Crane), was trustee for James M. Watson.

Name   : Moses   Owner: Durbin, Daniel
Date   : 1822/03/05   Page : 200
Bequeath: Durbin, Elizabeth
Relation: Wife

Name   : Moses   Owner: Saxon, Joshua
Date   : 1817/01/31   Page : 063
Bequeath: Saxon, Joshua
Relation: Son

Name   : Nad   Owner: Freeland, Frisby
Date   : 1817/??/??   Page : 081
Bequeath: Freeland, Thomas
Relation: Son

Name   : Nancy   Owner: Foster, William
Date   : 1812/02/10   Page : 038
Bequeath: Catrehead, Thebe
Relation: Daughter

Name   : Nancy   Owner: Saxon, Joshua
Date   : 1817/01/31   Page : 063
Bequeath: Saxon, Orville
Relation: Son

Name   : Nancy   Owner: Stampley, Jacob
Date   : 1829/06/02   Page : 162
Bequeath: Stampley, Nancy C.
Relation: Daughter

Name   : Nat   Owner: Thompson, John
Date   : 1833/03/30   Page : 290
Note: Nat was to remain on the John Thompson's farm.

Name   : Ned   Owner: Barnes, Joseph
Date   : 1821/04/08   Page : 134

NAMES FROM WILLBOOK

Ned(cont)
Bequeath: Barnes, Sarah
Relation: Sister

Name   : Ned   Owner: White, Thomas
Date   : 1808/02/18   Page : 008
Bequeath: Thomas, Sarah
Relation: Wife

Name   : Nedi   Owner: Gibson, Samual
Date   : 1817/11/24   Page : 079
Bequeath: Gibson, Joshua
Relation: Son
Husband : Vincent
Children: Bill, Burr, Lee and Jeremy.

Name   : Nell   Owner: Jenken,
                                   Phillips
Date   : 1819/11/29   Page : 212
Note: Emancipated.

Note   : Nelly   Owner: Jenken,
                                   Phillips
Date   : 1819/11/29   Page : 212
Bequeath: Elenor Hamilton's surviving child.

Name   : Nelson   Owner: Brashears,
                                   Turner
Date   : 1833/05/30   Page : 276
Bequeath: Brashears, Joseph
Relation: Son

Name   : New   Owner: Bullock, Mary
Date   : 1833/05/17   Page : 273
Parents : Billy and Patty.
Siblings: Jim, Flora, Alexander, Tenach, Rhoda,
          Vira, Melinda and Sarah.
Note: New was emancipated and sent to Libera with his parents and siblings.

Name   : Nina   Owner: Crane,
                                   Waterman
Date   : 1829/02/05   Page : 149
Bequeath: Crane, James

NAMES FROM WILLBOOK

Nina(cont)
Relation: Son
Note: Nina's children was also bequeathed to James Crane.

Name   : O'Young   Owner: Freeland,
                                  Frisby
Date   : 1817/??/??   Page : 081
Bequeath: Freeland, Augustus
Relation: Son

Name   : Orrie   Owner: Brashears,
                                  Turner
Date   : 1833/05/30   Page : 276
Bequeath: Brashears, Joseph
Relation: Son

Name   : Patience   Owner: Crane,
                                  Waterman
Date   : 1829/02/05   Page : 149
Bequeath: Watson, James M.
Relation: Grandson
Mother   : Dina
Siblings: Hary, Grace, Dan, Tora, Dick and Moses.
Note: William Young (son-in-law of Waterman Crane), was trustee for James M. Watson.

Name   : Patsy   Owner: Durbin, Daniel
Date   : 1822/03/05   Page : 200
Bequeath: Durbin, Elizabeth
Relation: Wife

Name   : Patsy   Owner: Roush, John
Date   : 1826/03/17   Page : 159
Note: Patsy was emancipated. The remaining of Roush's property went to John D. Zeizer.

Name   : Patty   Owner: Bullock, Mary
Date   : 1833/05/17   Page : 273
Husband : Billy
Children : Jim, Flora, Alexander, Tenach, Rhoda, New, Vira, Melinda and Sarah.

NAMES FROM WILLBOOK

Name   : Pegg   Owner: Thompson, John
Date   : 1833/03/30   Page : 290
Note: Pegg was to remain on John Thompson's farm.

Name   : Peggy   Owner: Barnes, Thomas
Date   : 1817/03/17   Page : 071
Bequeath: Barnes, Mary
Relation: Wife
Child   : Clorky

Name   : Peggy   Owner: Brashears,
                                     Turner
Date   : 1833/05/30   Page : 276
Bequeath: Brashears, Joseph
Relation: Son

Name   : Peggy   Owner: Moors, Robert
Date   : 1817/02/18   Page : 076
Bequeath: Robert Moor's Fiance.

Name   : Pellerand   Owner: Durbin, Daniel
Date   : 1822/03/05   Page : 200
Bequeath: Durbin, Elizabeth
Relation: Wife

Name   : Perry   Owner: Brisco, Thomas
Date   : 1830/04/18   Page : 232
Bequeath: Brisco, Virly
Relation: Wife

Name   : Peter   Owner: Bassett,
                                     William
Date   : 1820/05/24   Page : 128
Bequeath: Robinson, Jeremiah
Relation: Cousin

Name   : Peter   Owner: Barnes, Joseph
Date   : 1821/04/08   Page : 134
Bequeath: Barnes, Susan
Relation: Sister

Name   : Peter   Owner: Brashears,
Date   : 1814/04/16   Page: 051

NAMES FROM WILLBOOK

Peter(cont)
Note: Peter was Emancipated.

Name   : Peter   Owner: Green, Abram
Date   : 1826/06/02   Page : 168
Bequeath: Green, Andrew
Relation: Son
Child   : Eveline.
Note: Peter was the fther of Eveline.

Name   : Peter   Owner: Clabon, Harris
Date   : 1821/08/24   Page : 124
Bequeath: Clabon, Melvina
Relation: Daughter

Name   : Phebe   Owner: Brashears,
                                      Turner
Date   : 1833/05/30   Page : 276
Bequeath: Brashears, Joseph
Relation: Son

Name   : Phebe   Owner: Saxon, Joshua
Date   : 1817/01/31   Page : 063
Bequeath: Saxon, Milbourne
Relation: Son

Name   : Phil   Owner: Clark, Gibson
Date   : 1820/01/23   Page : 088
Bequeath: Clark, Susanah
Relation: Grandaughter

Name   : Phill   Owner: Brokus,
                                      William
Date   : 1805/10/05   Page : 016
Bequeath: Brokus, Ann
Relation: Wife

Name   : Phillip   Owner: Foster,
                                      William
Date   : 1812/02/10   Page : 038
Bequeath: Smith, Polly
Relation: ?

Name   : Phillip   Owner: Hanna, James

NAMES FROM WILLBOOK

Phillip(cont)
Date   : 1826/07/11   Page : 160
Bequeath: Draer, Jane
Relation: Sister

Name   : Phillis   Owner: Barnes, Esther
Date   : 1831/10/05   Page : 288
Bequeath: Barnes, Elias
Relation: Sister

Name   : Phillis   Owner: Barnes, Joseph
Date   : 1821/04/08   Page : 134
Bequeath: Barnes, Sarah
Relation: Sister

Name   : Pileey?   Owner: Freeland,
                                  Frisby
Date   : 1817/??/??   Page : 081
Bequeath: Freeland, Thomas
Relation: Son

Name   : Pilloy?   Owner: Freeland,
                                  Frisby
Date   : 1817/??/??   Page : 081
Bequeath: Freeland, August
Relation: Son

Name   : Pitcher   Owner: Brokus,
                                  William
Date   : 1805/10/05   Page : 016
Bequeath: Brokus, Ann
Relation: Wife

Name   : Polly   Owner: Thompson, John
Date   : 1833/03/30   Page : 290
Note: Polly was to remain on John Thompson's farm.

Name   : Pomp   Owner: Clabon, Harris
Date   : 1821/08/24   Page : 124
Bequeath: Clabon, Henderson
Relation: Son

Name   : Pompey   Owner: Saxon, Joshua

NAMES FROM WILLBOOK

Pompey(cont)
Date   : 1817/01/31   Page : 063
Bequeath: Anderson, Clarinda
Relation: Daughter

Name   : Posiba?   Owner: Bassett,
                                      William
Date   : 1820/05/24   Page : 128
Bequeath: Davis, Sarah
Relation: Cousin
Husband : Jim
Note: Posiba's five children were also
bequeathed to Sarah Davis.

Name   : Prince   Owner: Crane,
                                      Waterman
Date   : 1829/02/05   Page : 149
Bequeath: Crane, Catherine
Relation: Wife
Wife   : Sue
Children: John, Jacob, Lina and Eliza

Name   : Prissey   Owner: Freeland,
                                      Frisby
Date   : 1817/??/??   Page : 081
Bequeath: Freeland, Thomas
Relation: Son
Note: Prissey's children was also bequeathed
to Thomas Freeland.

Name   : Priscilla   Owner: Hanna, James
Date   : 1826/07/11   Page : 160
Bequeath: Dreaer, Jane
Relation: Son

Name   : Pyers   Owner: Bassett,
                                      William
Date   : 1820/05/24   Page : 128
Bequeath: Bassett, Huston
Relation: Brother

Name   : Rachael   Owner: Brashears,
                                      Marsham
Date   : 1831/01/17   Page : 230

NAMES FROM WILLBOOK

Rachael (cont)
Bequeath: Brashears, Turner
Relation: Son

Name   : Rachel   Owner: Brashears,
                                  Martha
Date   : 1814/04/16   Page : 051
Bequeath: Brashears, Marsham
Relation: Son

Name   : Rachel   Owner: Clark, Gibson
Date   : 1820/01/23   Page : 088
Note: Rachel was bequeathed to the children of Elijah Clark.

Name   : Rachel   Owner: Clarke, Lewis
Date   : 1825/10/30   Page : 206
Note: Rachel was to be sold.

Name   : Rachel   Owner: Durbin, Daniel
Date   : 1822/03/05   Page : 200
Bequeath: Durbin, Elizabeth
Relation: Wife

Name   : Rachel   Owner: Freeland,
                                  Frisby
Date   : 1817/??/??   Page : 081
Bequeath: Freeland, Augustus
Relation: Son

Name   : Rachel   Owner: Jenken,
                                  Phillips
Date   : 1819/11/29   Page : 212
Bequeath: Hunter, Mary
Relation: Granddaughter

Name   : Rachel   Owner: Saxon, Joshua
Date   : 1817/01/31   Page : 063
Note: Rachel was to be sold.

Name   : Rachel   Owner: Foster,
                                  William
Date   : 1812/02/10   Page : 038
Bequeath: Foster, Patsy

NAMES FROM WILLBOOK

Rachel (cont)
Relation: Daughter

Name   : Randell   Owner: Mundell,
                                      Andrew
Date   : 1817/01/23   Page : 069
Bequeath: Mundell, Abijah
Relation: Son

Name   : Rebecca   Owner: Durbin, Daniel
Date   : 1822/03/05   Page : 200
Bequeath: Easton, Zacariah
          Easton, Ann
Relation: ?
Note: Rebecca's children were also bequeathed
         to the Eastons.

Name   : Rhoda   Owner: Bullock, Mary
Date   : 1833/05/17   Page : 273
Parents : Billy and Patty.
Siblings: Jim, Flora, Alexander, Tenach, New,
          Vira, Melinda and Sarah.
Note: Rhoda was emancipated with her parents
         siblings and sent to Liberia.

Name   : Rhoda   Owner: Clarke, Lewis
Date   : 1825/10/30   Page : 206
Note: Rhoda was to be sold.

Name   : Rhoda   Owner: Stampley,
                                      Jacob
Date   : 1829/06/02   Page : 162
Bequeath: Stampley, Sarah
Relation: Daughter

Name   : Right   Owner: Brashears,
                                      Turner
Date   : 1833/05/30   Page : 276
Bequeath: Brashears, Joseph
Relation: Son

Name   : Robert   Owner: Brashears,
                                      Marsham
Date   : 1831/01/17   Page : 230

NAMES FROM WILLBOOK

Robert(cont)
Bequeath: Brashears, Turner
Relation: Son

Name   : Robin   Owner: Crane,
                                  Waterman
Date   : 1829/02/05   Page : 149
Bequeath: Crane, Catherine
Relation: Wife
Husband : Tan
Children : Washington and Mariah.

Name   : Russal   Owner: Durbin,
                                  Elizabeth
Date   : 1822/03/05   Page : 200
Bequeath: Durbin, Elizabeth
Relation: Wife

Name   : Rutland   Owner: Green, Abram
Date   : 1826/06/02   Page : 168
Bequeath: Green, Andrew
Relation: Son

Name   : Sabra   Owner: Brashears,
                                  Turner
Date   : 1833/05/30   Page : 276
Bequeath: Brashears, Amelia
Relation: Daughter

Name   : Salina   Owner: Barnes, Esther
Date   : 1831/10/05   Page : 288
Bequeath: Barnes, Elias
Relation: Son
Note: Salina's children were also bequeathed to Elias Barnes.

Name   : Sally   Owner: Crane,
                                  Waterman
Date   : 1829/02/05   Page : 149
Bequeath: Crane, Catherine
Relation: Wife
Father   : Sandy

Name   : Sally

NAMES FROM WILLBOOK

Sally (cont)
                                Owner: McCaleb,
                                       William
Date   : 1813/08/09   Page : 049
Bequeath: McCaleb, Ann
Relation: Wife
Child   : Emily

Name   : Sam   Owner: Barnes, Joseph
Date   : 1821/04/08   Page : 134
Bequeath: Barnes, Sarah
Relation: Son

Name   : Sam   Owner: Brashears,
                                   Marsham
Date   : 1831/01/17   Page : 230
Bequeath: Brashears, Turner
Relation: Son

Name   : Sam   Owner: Durbin, Daniel
Date   : 1822/03/05   Page : 200
Bequeath: Durbin, Elizabeth
Relation: Wife

Name   : Sam   Owner: Foster,
                                   William
Date   : 1812/02/10   Page : 038
Bequeath: Foster, Shadrack
Relation: Son

Name   : Sam   Owner: Phillip,
                                   Alston
Date   : 1827/05/17   Page: 203
  Note: Sam was to be emancipated three years after Phillip Alston's death or sold to the owner Sam requested.

Name   : Samual   Owner: Thompson, John
Date   : 1833/03/30   Page : 290
Note: Samual was to stay on John Thompson's farm.

Name   : Sandy   Owner: Crane,
                                   Waterman

NAMES FROM WILLBOOK

Sandy (cont)
Date   : 1829/02/05   Page : 149
Bequeath: Crane, Catherine
Relation: Wife
Child   : Sally

Name   : Sandy   Owner: Crane, Waterman
Date   : 1829/02/05   Page : 149
Bequeath: Crane, William
Relation: Grandson

Name   : Sarah   Owner: Brisco, Thomas
Date   : 1830/04/18   Page : 232
Bequeath: Brisco, Claiborne
Relation: Son

Name   : Sarah   Owner: Bullock, Mary
Date   : 1833/05/17   Page : 273
Parents : Billy and Patty.
Siblings: Jim, **Flora**, Alexander, Tenach, Rhoda, **New**, Viran and Melinda.
Note: Mary was emancipated and sent to Liberia with her parents and siblings.

Name   : Sarah   Owner: Durbin, Daniel
Date   : 1822/03/05   Page : 200
Bequeath: Durbin, Elizabeth
Relation: Wife

Name   : Sarah   Owner: Stampley, Jacob
Date   : 1829/06/02   Page : 162
Bequeath: Stampley, David
            Stampley, Samual
Relation: Son
Children: **Letty, Charlotte, Charles, Susey**.

Name   : Sarah   Owner: Stampley, Jacob
Date   : 1829/06/02   Page : 162
Bequeath: **Stampley, Sarah**
Relation: Daughter
Mother : Linda

NAMES FROM WILLBOOK

Name   : Sarah   Owner: Thomspon, John
Date   : 1833/03/30   Page : 290
Note: Sarah was to remain on John Thompson's farm.

Name   : Sarah Ann   Owner: Breazeale,
                                  Willis
Date   : 1833/05/30   Page : 234
Bequeath: Dan Allen
Mother   : Mary Ann
Sibling : Dan Allen
Note: Sarah's other siblings were not known.

Name   : Sarah Hill   Owner: Breazeale,
                                  Willis
Date   : 1822/05/30   Page : 234
Bequeath: Breazeale, Mary
Relation: Sister

Name   : Sasy   Owner: Cafferg, Mary
Date   : 1819/06/20   Page : 143
Bequeath: Walker, Rachel
Relation: Grandaughter

Name   : Sharper   Owner: Clabon, Harris
Date   : 1821/08/24   Page : 124
Bequeath: Clabon, Henderson
Relation: Son

Name   : Shed   Owner: Barnes, Joseph
Date   : 1821/04/08   Page : 134
Bequeath: Barnes, Susan
Relation: Sister

Name   : Sillah   Owner: Brashears,
                                  Martha
Date   : 1814/04/16   Page : 051
Bequeath: Brashears, Lea
Relation: Daughter

Name   : Sillah   Owner: Brashears,
                                  Turner
Date   : 1833/05/30   Page : 276
Bequeath: Brashears, Joseph

NAMES FROM WILLBOOK

Sillah(cont)
Relation: Son

Name   : Siloy   Owner: Cafferg, Mary
Date   : 1819/06/20   Page : 143
Bequeath: Cafferg, John
Relation: Son

Name   : Silva   Owner: Brashears,
                                  Martha
Date   1814/04/16   Page : 051
Bequeath: Brashears, Prisilla
Relation: Daughter
Mother   : Cloe
Sibling : Daphney

Name   : Silva   Owner: Brashears,
                                  Turner
Date   : 1833/05/30   Page : 276
Bequeath: Brashears, Joseph
Relation: Son

Name   : Sina   Owner: Green, Abram
Date   : 1826/06/02   Page : 168
Page   : Green, Andrew
Relation: Son

Name   : Sirus   Owner: Brokus,
                                  William
Date   : 1805/10/05   Page : 016
Bequeath: Brokus, Ann
Relation: Wife

Name   : Solomon   Owner: Barnes, Joseph
Date   : 1821/04/08   Page : 134
Bequeath: Barnes, Sarah
Relation: Sister

Name   : Solomon   Owner: Crane,
                                  Waterman
Date   : 1829/02/05   Page : 149
Bequeath: Quinn, Catherine
Relation: ?
Mother   : Lucinda

NAMES FROM WILLBOOK

Name   : Sophia   Owner: Cobun, Samuel
Date   : 1813/05/10   Page : 042
Bequeath: Cobun, Samuel
          Cobun, John
Relation: Sons

Name   : Sophy   Owner: Brashears,
                                         Marsham
Date   : 1831/01/17   Page : 230
Bequeath: Brashears, Turner
Relation: son

Name   : Stephen   Owner: Thompson, John
Date   : 1833/03/30   Page : 290
Note: Stephen was to stay on the John
Thompson's farm.

Name   : Suckey   Owner: Stampley,
                                         Jacob
Date   : 1829/06/02   Page : 162
Bequeath: Stampley, David
          Stampley, Samual
Relation: Sons

Name   : Sue   Owner: Crane,
                                         Waterman
Date   : 1829/02/05   Page : 149
Bequeath: Crane, Catherine
Relation: Wife
Husband : Prince
Children: John, Jacob, Lina and Elizabeth.

Name   : Susan   Owner: Brashears,
                                         Turner
Date   : 1833/05/30   Page : 276
Bequeath: Brashears, Amelia
Relation: Daughter

Name   : Susey   Owner: Stampley,
                                         Jacob
Date   : 1829/06/02   Page : 162
Bequeath: Stampley, David
          Stampley, Samual
Relation: Sons

NAMES FROM WILLBOOK

Susey (cont)
Mother   : Sarah
Siblings : Letty, Charlotte and Susey.

Name   : Tainey   Owner : Daniel, Ann
Date   : 1830/07/26   Page : 218
Bequeath : Morris, Ann
Relation : Daughter

Name   : Tan   Owner : Crane, Waterman
Date   : 1829/02/05   Page : 149
Bequeath : Crane, Catherine
Relation : Wife
Wife   : Robin
Children : Washington and Mariah.

Name   : Taney   Owner : Durbin, Daniel
Date   : 1822/03/05   Page : 200
Bequeath : Durbin, Elizabeth
Relation : Wife

Name   : Tarleton   Owner : Green, Abram
Date   : 1826/06/02   Page : 168
Bequeath : Green, Andrew
Relation : Son
Wife   : Evaline
Note: Their children were also bequeathed to Andrew Green.

Name   : Tenach   Owner : Bullock, Mary
Date   : 1833/05/17   Page : 273
Parents : Billy and Patty.
Siblings : Jim, Flora, Alexander, Rhoda, New, Vira, Melinda and Sarah.
Note: Tenach was emancipated with his parents and siblings and sent to Liberia.

Name   : Thomas   Owner : Durbin, Daniel
Date   : 1822/03/05   Page : 200
Bequeath : Durbin, Elizabeth
Relation : Wife

NAMES FROM WILLBOOK

Name   : Tiurbo   Owner: Brokus,
                                    William
Date   : 1805/10/05   Page : 016
Bequeath: Brokus, Ann
Relation: Wife

Name   : Tom   Owner: Barnes, Esther
Date   : 1831/10/05   Page : 288
Bequeath: Barnes, Elias
Relation: Son

Name   : Tom   Owner: Brashears,
                                    Martha
Date   : 1814/04/16   Page : 051
Bequeath: Brashears, Lea
Relation: Daughter

Name   : Tom   Owner: Freeland,
                                    Frisby
Date   : 1817/??/??   Page : 081
Bequeath: Freeland, Augustus
Relation: Son

Name   : Tom   Owner: Prescott, Abel
Bequeath: 1833/05/26   Page : 268
Mother   : Liza
Note: The amount due Abel Prescott from Evan Griffith was to be Given to Tom. He was to purchase his freedom.

Name   : Tom   Owner: Thompson, John
Date   : 1833/03/30   Page : 290
Note: Tom was to remain on the John Thompson's farm.

Name   : Tora   Owner: Crane,
                                    Waterman
Date   : 1829/02/05   Page : 149
Bequeath: Watson, James M.
Relation: Grandson
Mother   : Dina
Siblings: Hary, Grace, Dan, Dick, Patience,
          Moses.

NAMES FROM WILLBOOK

Tora(cont)
Note: William Young (son-in-law of Waterman Crane) was trustee for James M. Watson.

Name   : Vincent   Owner: Gibson, Samual
Date   : 1817/11/24   Page : 079
Bequeath: Gibson, Joshua
Relation: Son
Wife   : Nedi
Children: Bill, Burr, Lee and Jeremy.

Name   : Violet   Owner: Jenken, Phillips
Date   : 1819/11/29   Page : 212
Bequeath: Hunter, Hannah
Relation: Granddaughter

Name   : Vira   Owner: Bullock, Mary
Date   : 1833/05/17   Page : 273
Parents : Billy and Patty
Siblings: Jim, Flora, Alexander, Tenach, Rhoda, New, Melinda and Sarah.
Note: Vira was emancipated and sent to Liberia with her parents and siblings.
Vira's parents

Name   : Washingington   Owner: Crane, Waterman
Date   : 1829/02/05   Page : 149
Bequeath: Crane, Catherine
Relation: Wife
Parents : Tan
Sibling : Mariah

Name   : Washington   Owner: Green, Abram
Date   : 1826/06/02   Page : 168
Bequeath: unborn child

Name   : Wells   Owner: Crane, Waterman
Date   : 1829/02/05   Page : 149
Bequeath: Young, Clarissa
Relation: Daughter

NAMES FROM WILLBOOK

Name   : Will   Owner: Jenken,
                                      Phillips
Date   : 1819/11/29   Page : 212
Bequeath: Elenor Hamilton's surviving child.

Name   : Yenah   Owner: Barnes, Esther
Date   : 1831/10/05   Page : 288
Bequeath: Barnes, Elias
Relation: Son
Note: Yena's children were also bequeathed to
Elias Barnes.

PORT GIBSON PROPERTY
LIST 1846-1858

```
Name    : Aaron                          Age : 11
Owner   : Chambliss, Elizabeth And  Cortez
Year    : 1847/10/13                     Page: 063

Name    : Aaron                          Age : 6
Owner   : McGilvary, Mary And  Alexander
Year    : 1846/08/18                     Page: 030
Mother  : Rose
Siblings: Santre And Albert.

Name    : Abner                          Age : 5
Owner   : Frisby, Elizabeth And  Aaron
Year    : 1846/07/03                     Page: 010

Name    : Abraham                        Age : 9
Owner   : Coleman, Catharine And  John
Year    : 1857/04/18                     Page: 061

Name    : Abram                          Age : 28
Owner   : Snodgrass, Margaret And  John
Year    : 1846/08/24                     Page: 036

Name    : Absalom                        Age : 2
Owner   : Snodgrass, Margaret And  John
Year    : 1846/08/24                     Page: 036
Parents : Ferdinand and Mariah.
Siblings: Monroe and Edny.

Name    : Adaline                        Age : 19
Owner   : Spencer, Sarah A. And  H. W.
Year    : 1846/02/28                     Page: 008

Name    : Adam                           Age : 50
Owner   : Hamer, Amazon   And  William H.
Year    : 1846/08/01                     Page: 027
Note: Adam was born in Africa.

Name    : Adam                           Age : 50
Owner   : Wilson, Elizabeth And  Charles W.
Year    : 1846/07/31                     Page: 019

Name    : Adelaide                       Age : 4
Owner   : Deck, Julia Ann And  Alexander H.
```

PORT GIBSON PROPERTY
LIST 1846-1858

Adelaide(cont)
Year   : 1846/08/24   Page: 035
Mother   : Burdie

Name   : Adele   Age : 15
Owner   : McAlphine, Sally And William H.
Year   : 1854/01/01   Page: 077

Name   : Aggy   Age : ?
Owner   : Bland, Emeline   And Maxwell W.
Year   : 1846/08/04   Page: 024

Name   : Ailsey   Age : 10
Owner   : Buck, Maria   And William R.
Year   : 1846/08/27   Page: 038

Name   : Albert   Age : 2
Owner   : McGilvary, Mary And Alexander
Year   : 1846/08/18   Page: 030
Mother   : Rose
Siblings: Aaron And Santre.

Name   : Albert   Age : ?
Owner   : Mitchell, Harriet And John
Year   : 1857/09/22   Page: 061

Name   : Albert   Age : ?
Owner   : Stamps, Jane   And Volney
Year   : 1846/08/03   Page: 021
Mother   : Eliza
Siblings: Junius, Crockett, Humphreys, Victoria
          and Ina.

Name   : Alfred   Age : ?
Owner   : Bland, Emeline   And Maxwell W.
Year   : 1846/08/04   Page: 024

Name   : Alice   Age : 22
Owner   : McAlphine, Sally And William H.
Year   : 1854/01/01   Page: 077

Name   : Alice   Age : 3
Owner   : Thomson, Caroline And Benjamin W.

54

PORT GIBSON PROPERTY
LIST 1846-1858

Alice(cont)
Year   : 1846/08/04   Page: 041
Parents : Buck And Emily.
Siblings: Joe, Andrew and Mary.

Name : Allen   Age : 1
Owner : McIntyre, Emily And Thomas G.
Year : 1848/01/15   Page: 045

Name : Allen   Age : 27
Owner : Moore, Permelia And Rich M.
Year : 1846/07/18   Page: 015

Name : Allice   Age : ?
Owner : Patton, Malinda And Francis
Year : 1846/06/26   Page: 006

Name : Allice   Age : ?
Owner : Rossman, Hariet And Dr. Walter
Year : 1846/07/21   Page: 017

Name : Allick   Age : 33
Owner : Clarke, Martha And Elijah L.
Year : 1846/02/28   Page: 031
Note: Allick was the property of the William Ervin Estate.

Name   : Allis   Age : 2
Owner   : Brock, Vashti And Valentine
Year   : 1848/05/23   Page: 048
Mother : Lucinda
Sibling : Louisa
Note: Vashti was heir of A. Brook from Louisiana.

Name : Alnisa   Age : 9
Owner : O'Kelly, Hester And William
Year : 1850/04/27   Page: 054

Name : Amanda   Age : 10
Owner : Frisby, Elizabeth And Aaron
Year : 1846/07/03   Page: 010

PORT GIBSON PROPERTY LIST 1846-1858

Name   : Amelia   Age : 1
Owner   : McIntyre, Emily And Thomas G.
Year   : 1848/01/15   Page: 045

Name   : Americus   Age : 5
Owner   : Shaifer, Elizabeth And Abram K.
Year   : 1846/06/10   Page: 003
Parents : William And Mary
Siblings: Cyrus, Suzette and Mary Ann.

Name   : Amos   Age : 3
Owner   : Sillers, Caroline And William
Year   : 1846/07/22   Page: 018
Mother : Cely
Siblings: Wash, Ebb, Park, Mary, Betsy and Hester.

Name   : Amus   Age : 8
Owner   : Hamer, Amazon And William H.
Year   : 1846/08/01   Page: 027

Name   : Amy   Age : 35
Owner   : Brown, Ann And Thomas W.
Year   : 1846/04/29   Page: 001
Note   : Ann Brown was heir of Ralph Regan.

Name   : Amy   Age : 22
Owner   : Sillers, Caroline And William
Year   : 1846/07/22   Page: 018
Child   : Charlotte.

Name   : Amy   Age : 40
Owner   : Wilson, Elizabeth And Charles W.
Year   : 1846/07/31   Page: 019

Name   : Anderson   Age : 11
Owner   : Coleman, Catharine And John
Year   : 1857/04/18   Page: 061

Name   : Andrew   Age : ?
Owner   : Bland, Emeline And Maxwell W.
Year   : 1846/08/04   Page: 024

Name   : Andrew   Age : 8

PORT GIBSON PROPERTY
LIST 1846-1858

Andrew(cont)
Owner   : McDougall, Ann E. And Duncan
Year   : 1846/07/02   Page: 006

Name   : Andrew   Age : 17
Owner   : McIntyre, Emily And Thomas G.
Year   : 1848/01/15   Page: 045

Name   : Andrew   Age : 12
Owner   : McIntyre, Emily And Thomas G.
Year   : 1848/01/15   Page: 045

Name   : Andrew   Age : 10
Owner   : Spencer, Sarah A. And H. W.
Year   : 1846/02/28   Page: 008

Name   : Andrew   Age : 6
Owner   : Thomson, Caroline And Benjamin W.
Year   : 1846/08/04   Page: 041
Parents : Buck And Emily.
Siblings: Joe, Alice and Mary.

Name   : Ann   Age : 3
Owner   : Brown, Ann   And Thomas W.
Year   : 1846/04/29   Page: 001
Note: Ann Brown was heir of Ralph Regan.

Name   : Ann   Age : 19
Owner   : Buck, Maria   And William R.
Year   : 1846/08/27   Page: 038

Name   : Ann   Age : 20
Owner   : Chambliss, Elizabeth And Cortez
Year   : 1847/10/13   Page: 063

Name   : Ann   Age : 45
Owner   : Marye, Mary P.   And James T.
Year   : 1848/05/06   Page: 048

Name   : Ann   Age : ?
Owner   : Mitchell, Harriet And John
Year   : 1857/09/22   Page: 061

PORT GIBSON PROPERTY LIST 1846-1858

Name : Ann   Age : ?
Owner : Mitchell, Harriet And John
Year : 1857/09/22   Page: 061

Name : Ann   Age : 1
Owner : Shaifer, Clarissa And Henry T.
Year : 1852/06/24   Page: 062

Name : Ann   Age : 30
Owner : Wilson, Elizabeth And Charles W.
Year : 1846/07/31   Page: 019

Name : Anne   Age : ?
Owner : Bland, Emeline And Maxwell W.
Year : 1846/08/04   Page: 024

Name : Anthony   Age : 22
Owner : Clarke, Martha And Elijah L.
Year : 1846/02/28   Page: 031
Note: Anthony was the property of the William Ervin Estate.

Name : Arch   Age : 11
Owner : Clarke, Martha And Elijah L.
Year : 1846/02/28   Page: 031
Note: Arch was the property of the William Ervin Estate.

Name : Areodine   Age : 5
Owner : Coleman, Catharine And John
Year : 1857/04/18   Page: 061

Name : Arnette   Age : 5
Owner : Moore, Permelia And Rich M.
Year : 1846/07/18   Page: 015
Note: Mulatto.

Name : Arnold   Age : 30
Owner : McIntyre, Emily And Thomas G.
Year : 1848/01/15   Page: 045

Name : Aruelia   Age : 4
Owner : Spencer, Sarah A. And H. W.

PORT GIBSON PROPERTY
LIST 1846-1858

Aruelia(cont)
Year   : 1846/02/28   Page: 008
Mother : Cynthia
Sibling : Ellen, Cora, Priscilla and Jeffrey.

Name : Augustus   Age : 20
Owner : McIntyre, Emily And Thomas G.
Year : 1848/01/15   Page: 045

Name : Austin   Age : ?
Owner : Patton, Malinda And Francis
Year : 1846/06/26   Page: 006

Name : Becca   Age : 28
Owner : Brown, Ann   And Thomas W.
Year : 1846/04/29   Page: 001
Note: Ann Brown was heir of Ralph Regan.

Name : Becca   Age : 12
Owner : McIntyre, Emily And Thomas G.
Year : 1848/01/15   Page: 045

Name : Ben   Age : 4
Owner : Frisby, Elizabeth And Aaron
Year : 1846/07/03   Page: 010

Name : Ben   Age : 25
Owner : Shaifer, Elizabeth And Abram K.
Year : 1846/06/10   Page: 003

Name : Bess   Age : 14
Owner : McIntyre, Emily And Thomas G.
Year : 1848/01/15   Page: 045

Name : Bets   Age : ?
Owner : Patton, Malinda And Francis
Year : 1846/06/26   Page: 006

Name : Betsey   Age : 40
Owner : Brown, Ann   And Thomas W.
Year : 1846/04/29   Page: 001
Note: Ann Brown was heir of Ralph Regan.
Betsey was called "Big" Betsey.

PORT GIBSON PROPERTY
LIST 1846-1858

Name   : Betsey   Age : 19
Owner : McIntyre, Emily And Thomas G.
Year   : 1848/01/15   Page: 045

Name   : Betsy   Age : 7
Owner : Brown, Ann   And Thomas W.
Year   : 1846/04/29   Page: 001
Parents: Shadrack And Nicey.
Siblings: Sophia
Note: Ann Brown was heir of Ralph Regan.
Betsy was called "Little" Betsy.

Name   : Betsy   Age : 26
Owner : Patterson, Louise And James H.
Year   : 1854/05/02   Page: 074
Children: Jane and Julia.
Note: Betsy was conveyed in 1854 by Theophedus and Nancy Eddins December 27 1849 and recorded in Book Z, Page 1, Clerk Of The Propate Court, Claiborne County.

Name   : Betsy   Age : 9
Owner : Sillers, Caroline And William
Year   : 1846/07/22   Page: 018
Mother : Cely
Siblings: Wash, Ebb, Park, Mary, Hester and Amos.

Name   : Biddy   Age : 10
Owner : Buck, Maria   And William R.
Year   : 1846/08/27   Page: 038

Name   : Bill   Age : 5
Owner : Bobo, Eliza M.   And Absalom H.
Year   : 1846/08/12   Page: 029
Mother : Ellen
Sibling : Raney

Name   : Bill   Age : 40
Owner : Brock, Vashti And Valentine W.
Year   : 1848/05/23   Page: 048
Wife   : Rose
Note: Vashti was heir of A. Brook from Louisiana.

PORT GIBSON PROPERTY
LIST 1846-1858

```
Name   : Bill                        Age : 16
Owner  : Buck, Maria      And  William R.
Year   : 1846/08/27                  Page: 038

Name   : Bill                        Age : 16
Owner  : Marye, Mary P.   And  James T.
Year   : 1848/05/06                  Page: 048

Name   : Bill                        Age : 2
Owner  : McIntyre, Emily  And  Thomas G.
Year   : 1848/01/15                  Page: 045

Name    : Bill                       Age : 40
Owner   : Sillers, Caroline And William
Year    : 1846/07/22                 Page: 018
Wife    : Mary Ann
Children: Van Buren, Ralph Jr and Joseph.

Name   : Billy                       Age : 10
Owner  : Brown, Ann       And  Thomas W.
Year   : 1854/08/09                  Page: 076

Name   : Billy                       Age : 4
Owner  : Chambliss, Elizabeth And Cortez
Year   : 1847/10/13                  Page: 063

Name    : Billy                      Age : ?
Owner   : Stamps, Jane     And  Volney
Year    : 1846/08/03                 Page: 021
Mother  : Sarah
Sibling : Kate

Name   : Bob                         Age : ?
Owner  : Bland, Emeline   And  Maxwell W.
Year   : 1846/08/04                  Page: 024

Name   : Bob                         Age : 35
Owner  : McIntyre, Emily  And  Thomas G.
Year   : 1848/01/15                  Page: 045

Name   : Bob                         Age : ?
Owner  : Patton, Malinda  And  Francis
Year   : 1846/06/26                  Page: 006
```

PORT GIBSON PROPERTY LIST 1846-1858

Name   : Braim   Age : 12
Owner   : McIntyre, Emily And Thomas G.
Year   : 1848/01/15   Page: 045

Name   : Buck   Age : 45
Owner   : Thomson, Caroline And Benjamin W.
Year   : 1846/08/04   Page: 041
Wife   : Emily
Children : Joe, Andrew, Alice and Mary.

Name   : Burdie   Age : 22
Owner   : Deck, Julia Ann And Alexander H.
Year   : 1846/08/24   Page: 035
Child   : Adelaide
Note: Mulatto.

Name   : Caleb   Age : 3
Owner   : McIntyre, Emily And Thomas G.
Year   : 1848/01/15   Page: 045

Name   : Caleb   Age : 20
Owner   : Spencer, Sarah A. And H. W.
Year   : 1846/02/28   Page: 008

Name   : Caleb   Age : 14
Owner   : Spencer, Sarah A And H. W.
Year   : 1846/02/28   Page: 008

Name   : Calvin   Age : 3
Owner   : McIntyre, Emily And Thomas G.
Year   : 1848/01/15   Page: 045

Name   : Camilleo   Age : 8
Owner   : McIntyre, Emily And Thomas G.
Year   : 1848/01/15   Page: 045

Name   : Caroline   Age : ?
Owner   : Chambliss, Mary And Calvin T.
Year   : 1852/08/09   Page: 066

Name   : Caroline   Age : 18
Owner   : Davidson, Sarah And Curvan
Year   : 1853/03/18   Page: 069

PORT GIBSON PROPERTY
LIST 1846-1858

Name   : Caroline   Age : 20
Owner   : McAlphine, Sally And William H.
Year   : 1854/01/01   Page: 077

Name   : Caroline   Age : 22
Owner   : McDougall, Elizabeth And Nicholas
Year   : 1847/08/09   Page: 043

Name   : Caroline   Age : 28
Owner   : McGilvary, Mary And Alexander
Year   : 1846/08/18   Page: 030
Children: Charles, Henry and Lucy.

Name   : Caroline   Age : 24
Owner   : Moore, Permelia And Rich M.
Year   : 1846/07/18   Page: 015

Name   : Caroline   Age : 25
Owner   : Sayer, Harriet B. And William D.
Year   : 1847/03/03   Page: 041

Name   : Caroline   Age : 19
Owner   : Spencer, Sarah A. And H. W.
Year   : 1846/02/28   Page: 008

Name   : Carrol   Age : 2
Owner   : Moore, Permelia And Rich M.
Year   : 1846/07/18   Page: 015
Note: Boy.

Name   : Carroll   Age : 30
Owner   : Gage, Rosanna And James A.
Year   : 1846/07/20   Page: 016
Note: Man.

Name   : Carter   Age : 6
Owner   : Brown, Ann   And Thomas W.
Year   : 1846/04/29   Page: 001
Note: Ann Brown Was Heir Of Ralph Regan.

Name   : Catharine   Age : ?
Owner   : Chambliss, Mary And Calvin T.
Year   : 1852/08/09   Page: 066

63

PORT GIBSON PROPERTY LIST 1846-1858

Name   : Catharine   Age : 8
Owner   : Rivers, Mary W. And Orville C.
Year   : 1851/04/10   Page: 058
Mother : Lucy,
Sibling : Catharine And Mary.

Name : Cato   Age : 18
Owner : McIntyre, Emily And Thomas G.
Year : 1848/01/15   Page: 045

Name : Caty   Age : 12
Owner : Snodgrass, Margaret And John
Year : 1846/08/24   Page: 036

Name : Ceasar   Age : 32
Owner : Snodgrass, Margaret And John
Year : 1846/08/24   Page: 036

Name   : Cely   Age : 47
Owner   : Sillers, Caroline And William
Year   : 1846/07/22   Page: 018
Children : Wash, Ebb, Park, Mary, Betsy, Hester and Amos.

Name : Cetty   Age : 40
Owner : Griffins, Sarah And Francis
Year : 1850/07/08   Page: 057

Name   : Chaney   Age : 3
Owner   : Snodgrass, Margaret And John
Year   : 1846/08/24   Page: 036
Mother   : Harriet Ann
Siblings : Clem And Olevia.

Name : Chany   Age : 25
Owner : Frisby, Elizabeth And Aaron
Year : 1846/07/03   Page: 010

Name : Chany   Age : 28
Owner : Griffins, Sarah And Francis
Year : 1851/02/18   Page: 058
Child : Cynthia.

64

PORT GIBSON PROPERTY
LIST 1846-1858

Name   : Chapurnur   Age : ?
Owner   : Brock, Vashti And Valentine W.
Year   : 1848/05/23   Page: 048
Mother : Eliza
Sibling : Mariah, Matilda, Courtney, Elizabeth
Note: Vashti was heir of A. Brook from Louisiana.

Name   : Charity   Age : 25
Owner   : Brown, Ann   And Thomas W.
Year   : 1846/04/29   Page: 001
Note: Charity was related to Willis, Henry And Jony. Ann Brown was heir of Ralph Regan.

Name   : Charity   Age : 36
Owner   : Clarke, Martha And Elijah L.
Year   : 1846/02/28   Page: 031

Name   : Charity   Age : 35
Owner   : Griffins, Sarah And Francis
Year   : 1851/02/18   Page: 058

Name   : Charles   Age : 10
Owner   : Brock, Vashti And Valentine W.
Year   : 1848/05/23   Page: 048
Mother : Irene
          Vashti was heir of A. Brook from Louisiana.

Name   : Charles   Age : 19
Owner   : Brown, Ann   And Thomas W.
Year   : 1846/04/29   Page: 001
Note: Charles was related to Jake, Mary And Jesse. Ann Brown was heir of Ralph Regan. Charles was called "Little" Charles.

Name   : Charles   Age : 34
Owner   : Brown, Ann   And Thomas W.
Year   : 1846/04/29   Page: 001
Note: Ann Brown was heir of Ralph Regan. Charles was Called "Big" Charles.

Name   : Charles   Age : 38

PORT GIBSON PROPERTY
LIST 1846-1858

Charles (cont)
Owner : Coleman, Catharine And John
Year : 1857/04/18   Page: 061

Name : Charles   Age : 9
Owner : Coleman, Catharine And John
Year : 1857/04/18   Page: 061

Name   : Charles   Age : 8
Owner : McGilvary, Mary And Alexander
Year   : 1846/08/18   Page: 030
Mother : Caroline
Sibling : Henry And Lucy.

Name : Charlotte   Age : 40
Owner : McIntyre, Emily And Thomas G.
Year : 1848/01/15   Page: 045

Name   : Charlotte   Age : 1
Owner : Porter, Elizabeth And D. R.
Year   : 1854/05/24   Page: 075
Mother : Martha
Sibling : Matilda
Note: Charlotte was purchased from T.F. Lindsey
On January 4, 1851.

Name : Charlotte   Age : 30
Owner : Sayer, Harriet B. And William D.
Year : 1847/03/03   Page: 041

Name   : Charlotte   Age : 2
Owner : Sillers, Caroline And William
Year   : 1846/07/22   Page: 018
Mother : Amy.

Name : Charlotte   Age : 19
Owner : Sims, Emeline F. And Isaac A.
Year : 1847/03/25   Page: 042

Name : Christian   Age : 28
Owner : McIntyre, Emily And Thomas G.
Year : 1848/01/15   Page: 045

PORT GIBSON PROPERTY
LIST 1846-1858

```
Name   : Claiborne                       Age : 22
Owner  : Buck, Maria        And  William R.
Year   : 1846/08/27                      Page: 038

Name   : Clarisa                         Age : 35
Owner  : Gordon, Candis     And  Johnson W.
Year   : 1846/08/03                      Page: 022

Name   : Clarissa                        Age : 4
Owner  : McIntyre, Emily    And  Thomas G.
Year   : 1848/01/15                      Page: 045

Name   : Clea                            Age : 37
Owner  : Frisby, Elizabeth  And  Aaron
Year   : 1846/07/03                      Page: 010

Name   : Clem                            Age : 5
Owner  : Snodgrass, Margaret And  John
Year   : 1846/08/24                      Page: 036
Mother : Harriet Ann
Sibling: Chaney And Olevia.

Name   : Cleone                          Age : 80
Owner  : Coleman, Catharine And  John
Year   : 1857/04/18                      Page: 061

Name   : Clia                            Age : 2
Owner  : McIntyre, Emily    And  Thomas G.
Year   : 1848/01/15                      Page: 045

Name   : Conny                           Age : 2
Owner  : Snodgrass, Margaret And  John
Year   : 1846/08/24                      Page: 036
Mother : Harriet N.
Sibling: George.

Name   : Cora                            Age : 7
Owner  : Spencer, Sarah A.  And  H. W.
Year   : 1846/02/28                      Page: 008
Mother : Cynthia
Sibling: Ellen, Aruelia, Priscilla.

Name   : Courtney                        Age : ?
```

PORT GIBSON PROPERTY
LIST 1846-1858

Courtney(cont)
Owner   : Brock, Vashti And Valentine W.
Year   : 1848/05/23   Page: 048
Mother   : Eliza
Siblings : Mariah, Matilda, Hariet, Sam,
           Chapurnur and Elizabeth.
Note: Vashti was heir of A. Brook From
Louisiana.

Name   : Crack   Age : 7
Owner   : Sims, Emeline F. And Isaac A.
Year   : 1847/03/25   Page: 042
Parents : Sam And Sylva
Siblings : Little Fanny, Manda and Infant 6
           months old.

Name   : Crawford   Age : 2
Owner   : Magrunder, Sarah And Dr. Thomas B.
Year   : 1852/08/14   Page: 067

Name   : Creasy   Age : ?
Owner   : Strong, Malinda And George P.
Year   : 1846/05/30   Page: 004

Name   : Crockett   Age : ?
Owner   : Stamps, Jane And Volney
Year   : 1846/08/03   Page: 021
Mother   : Eliza
Sibling : Junius, Humphreys, Irene, Al,
           Victoria and Ina.

Name   : Cuff   Age : ?
Owner   : Bland, Emeline And Maxwell W.
Year   : 1846/08/04   Page: 024

Name   : Cynth   Age : 50
Owner   : Shaifer, Clarissa And Henry T.
Year   : 1852/06/24   Page: 062

Name   : Cyntha   Age : 3
Owner   : Griffins, Sarah And Francis
Year   : 1851/02/18   Page: 058
Mother   : Chany.

PORT GIBSON PROPERTY LIST 1846-1858

Name   : Cynthia   Age : 27
Owner   : Spencer, Sarah A. And H. W.
Year   : 1846/02/28   Page: 008
Children: Ellen, Cora, Aruelia, Priscilla
          and Jeffrey.

Name   : Cynthy   Age : 5
Owner   : Snodgrass, Margaret And John
Year   : 1846/08/24   Page: 036

Name   : Cyrus   Age : 19
Owner   : Shaifer, Elizabeth And Abram K.
Year   : 1846/06/10   Page: 003
Parents : William and Mary.
Siblings: Suzette, Amerricus and Mary Ann.

Name   : Dabney   Age : 5
Owner   : Coleman, Catharine And John
Year   : 1857/04/18   Page: 061

Name   : Dafney   Age : ?
Owner   : Patton, Malinda And Francis
Year   : 1846/06/26   Page: 006

Name   : Daniel   Age : ?
Owner   : Patton, Malinda And Francis
Year   : 1846/06/26   Page: 006

Name   : Darcus   Age : 14
Owner   : Spencer, Sarah A. And H. W.
Year   : 1846/02/28   Page: 008

Name   : Dave   Age : 3
Owner   : Clarke, Martha And Elijah L.
Year   : 1846/02/28   Page: 031
Note: Slaves were the property of The
William Ervin Estate.

Name   : Dave   Age : 26
Owner   : Griffins, Sarah And Francis
Year   : 1851/02/18   Page: 058

Name   : Dave   Age : ?

PORT GIBSON PROPERTY LIST 1846-1858

Dave(cont)
Owner : Patton, Malinda And Francis
Year : 1846/06/26   Page: 006

Name : Dave   Age : 10
Owner : Thomson, Elizabeth And Thomas W.
Year : 1846/07/02   Page: 013

Name : Delia   Age : 7
Owner : Coleman, Catharine And John
Year : 1857/04/18   Page: 061

Name : Demps   Age : 19
Owner : McAlphine, Sally And William H.
Year : 1854/01/01   Page: 077

Name   : Dennis   Age : 2
Owner : Thomson, Caroline And Benjamin W.
Year   : 1851/02/12   Page: 056
Mother : Milly.

Name : Diana   Age : 25
Owner : Buck, Maria   And William R.
Year : 1846/08/27   Page: 038

Name : Dicey   Age : 14
Owner : McIntyre, Emily And Thomas G.
Year : 1848/01/15   Page: 045

Name : Dick   Age : 37
Owner : Chambliss, Elizabeth And Cortez
Year : 1847/10/13   Page: 063

Name : Dick   Age : 30
Owner : Sayer, Harriet B. And William D.
Year : 1847/03/03   Page: 041

Name   : Dick   Age : 44
Owner   : Sillers, Caroline And William
Year   : 1846/02/08   Page: 017
Wife   : Lucy,
Children : Gold, Smith, Huldah and Louise.

PORT GIBSON PROPERTY
LIST 1846-1858

Name   : Dilcey   Age : ?
Owner   : Patton, Malinda   And Francis
Year   : 1846/06/26   Page: 006

Name   : Diller   Age : ?
Owner   : Mitchell, Harriet And John
Year   : 1857/09/22   Page: 061

Name   : Dinah   Age : 13
Owner   : Clarke, Martha   And Elijah L.
Year   : 1846/02/28   Page: 031
Note: Slaves were the property of The
William Ervin Estate.

Name   : Dinah   Age : 48
Owner   : Posey, Sarah   And Humphrey M.
Year   : 1846/07/04   Page: 007

Name   : Earline   Age : 21
Owner   : Shaifer, Clarissa And Henry T.
Year   : 1852/06/24   Page: 062

Name   : Easter   Age : .3
Owner   : Brown, Ann   And Thomas W.
Year   : 1846/04/29   Page: 001
Note: Ann Brown was heir of Ralph Regan.

Name   : Ebb   Age : 14
Owner   : Sillers, Caroline And William
Year   : 1846/07/22   Page:
Mother : Cely
Sibling : Wash, Park, Mary, Betsy, Hester?

Name   : Edmond   Age : ?
Owner   : Patton, Malinda   And Francis
Year   : 1846/06/26   Page: 006

Name   : Edny   Age : 1
Owner   : Snodgrass, Margaret And John
Year   : 1846/08/24   Page: 036
Parents : Ferdinand and Mariah.
Sibling : Monroe And ?

PORT GIBSON PROPERTY
LIST 1846-1858

Name   : Edy   Age : 3
Owner : McIntyre, Emily And Thomas G.
Year   : 1848/01/15   Page: 045

Name   : Elam   Age : 3
Owner : Coleman, Catharine And John
Year   : 1857/04/18   Page: 061

Name   : Elam   Age : 10
Owner : McDougall, Ann E. And Duncan
Year   : 1846/07/02   Page: 006

Name   : Elijah   Age : 10
Owner : McIntyre, Emily And Thomas G.
Year   : 1848/01/15   Page: 045

Name   : Eliza   Age : 46
Owner   : Brock, Vashti And Valentine W.
Year   : 1848/05/23   Page: 048
Children: Mariah, Matilda, Courtney, Hariet,
          Sam, Chapurner and Elizabeth.
Note: Vashti was heir of A. Brook from
Louisiana. Children ages are from six
months to of age.

Name   : Eliza   Age : 46
Owner : Chambliss, Elizabeth And Cortez
Year   : 1847/10/13   Page: 063

Name   : Eliza   Age : 1
Owner : McIntyre, Emily And Thomas G.
Year   : 1848/01/15   Page: 045

Name   : Eliza   Age : ?
Owner : Mitchell, Harriet And John
Year   : 1857/09/22   Page: 061

Name   : Eliza   Age : ?
Owner : Mitchell, Harriet And John
Year   : 1857/09/22   Page: 061

Name   : Eliza   Age : .6
Owner : Rivers, Mary W. And Orville C.

PORT GIBSON PROPERTY
LIST 1846-1858

Eliza(cont)
Year   : 1851/04/10   Page: 058
Mother   : Lucy
Siblings : Catharine and Mary.

Name   : Eliza   Age : 6
Owner : Sayer, Harriet B. And William D.
Year   : 1847/03/03   Page: 041

Name   : Eliza   Age : ?
Owner   : Stamps, Jane   And Volney
Year   : 1846/08/03   Page: 021
Children : Junis, Crockett, Humphreys, Irene,
           Albert, Victoria and Ina.

Name   : Elizabeth   Age : ?
Owner   : Brock, Vashti and Valentine W.
Year   : 1848/05/23   Page: 048
Mother   : Eliza
Siblings : Mariah, Matilda, Courtney, Hariet,
           Sam and Chapurnur.
Note: Vashti was heir of A. Brook from
Louisiana.

Name   : Elizabeth   Age : 30
Owner   : Brock, Vashti And Valentine W.
Year   : 1848/05/23   Page: 048
Note: Vashti was heir of A. Brook from
Louisiana.
Children : Elizabeth and Josephine.

Name   : Elizabeth   Age : 6
Owner   : Brock, Vashti and Valentine W.
Year   : 1848/05/23   Page: 048
Mother   : Millly
Sibling : Josephine
Note: Vashti was heir of A. Brook from
Louisiana.

Name   : Elizabeth   Age : ?
Owner : Mitchell, Harriet And John
Year   : 1857/09/22   Page: 061

PORT GIBSON PROPERTY
LIST 1846-1858

Name   : Elizabeth   Age : 13
Owner : Patterson, Louise And James H.
Year   : 1854/05/02   Page: 074
Note: Conveyed by Theophidus and Nancy Eddins December 27 1849 and recorded in Book Z, Page 1, Clerk Of The Propate Court, Claiborne County.

Name   : Elizabeth   Age : ?
Owner : Rossman, Hariet And Dr. Walter
Year   : 1846/07/21   Page: 017

Name   : Ella   Age : .6
Owner : McIntyre, Emily And Thomas G.
Year   : 1848/01/15   Page: 045

Name   : Ellen   Age : ?
Owner : Bland, Emeline   And Maxwell W.
Year   : 1846/08/04   Page: 024

Name   : Ellen   Age : 26
Owner : Bobo, Eliza M.   And Absalom H.
Year   : 1846/08/12   Page: 029
Children: Bill And Raney.

Name   : Ellen   Age : 25
Owner : Buck, Maria   And William R.
Year   : 1846/08/27   Page: 038

Name   : Ellen   Age : 15
Owner : Coleman, Catharine And John
Year   : 1857/04/18   Page: 061

Name   : Ellen   Age : 26
Owner : McIntyre, Emily And Thomas G.
Year   : 1848/01/15   Page: 045

Name   : Ellen   Age : 9
Owner : Spencer, Sarah A. And H. W.
Year   : 1846/02/28   Page: 008
Mother : Cynthia
Siblings: Cora, Aruelia, Priscilla and Jeffrey.

PORT GIBSON PROPERTY
LIST 1846-1858

```
Name    : Ellen                       Age  : ?
Owner   : Tebo, Ann C.     And  William B.
Year    : 1846/06/27                  Page: 013
Note: Ellen had a Child.

Name    : Ellick                      Age  : 35
Owner   : Wilson, Elizabeth And  Charles W.
Year    : 1846/07/31                  Page: 017

Name    : Elsey                       Age  : 7
Owner   : McDougall, Susan And  Daniel
Year    : 1853/02/02                  Page: 070
Mother  : Sarah
Sibling : Lucy.
Note: Mulatto.

Name    : Elsey                       Age  : 15
Owner   : McIntyre, Emily  And  Thomas G.
Year    : 1848/01/15                  Page: 045

Name    : Elvira                      Age  : 8
Owner   : Brown, Ann       And  Thomas W.
Year    : 1846/04/29                  Page: 001
Note: Ann Brown was heir of Ralph Regan.

Name    : Emaline                     Age  : 17
Owner   : Brown, Ann       And  Thomas W.
Year    : 1854/08/09                  Page: 076

Name    : Emanuel                     Age  : 3
Owner   : McIntyre, Emily  And  Thomas G.
Year    : 1848/01/15                  Page: 045

Name    : Emily                       Age  : 14
Owner   : Gordon, Candis   And  Johnson W.
Year    : 1846/08/03                  Page: 022
Note: Mulatto.

Name    : Emily                       Age  : ?
Owner   : Patton, Malinda  And  Francis
Year    : 1846/06/26                  Page: 006

Name    : Emily                       Age  : 35
```

PORT GIBSON PROPERTY
LIST 1846-1858

Emily(cont)
Owner : Sayer, Harriet B. And William D.
Year : 1847/03/03   Page: 041

Name : Emily   Age : 19
Owner : Shaifer, Elizabeth And Abram K.
Year : 1846/06/10   Page: 003

Name : Emily   Age : 40
Owner : Thomson, Caroline And Benjamin W.
Year : 1852/06/14   Page: 065
Child : Tom.

Name : Ephraim   Age : 12
Owner : Brown, Ann   And Thomas W.
Year : 1854/08/09   Page: 076

Name : Ephraim   Age : 13
Owner : Griffins, Sarah And Francis
Year : 1851/02/18   Page: 058

Name : Esther   Age : 40
Owner : Buck, Maria   And William R.
Year : 1846/08/27   Page: 038

Name : Eveline   Age : ?
Owner : Bland, Emeline And Maxwell W.
Year : 1846/08/04   Page: 024

Name : Eveline   Age : 30
Owner : McIntyre, Emily And Thomas G.
Year : 1848/01/15   Page: 045

Name : Fanny   Age : 4
Owner : Marye, Mary P. And James T.
Year : 1846/08/18   Page: 032

Name : Fanny   Age : 35
Owner : McIntyre, Emily And Thomas G.
Year : 1848/01/15   Page: 045

Name : Fanny   Age : ?
Owner : Patton, Malinda And Francis

PORT GIBSON PROPERTY
LIST 1846-1858

Fanny(cont)
Year   : 1846/06/26   Page: 006

Name   : Fanny   Age : 40
Owner   : Sims, Emeline F. And Isaac A.
Year   : 1846/10/25   Page: 042
Husband   : Monk.

Name   : Fanny   Age : 9
Owner   : Sims, Emeline F. And Isaac A.
Year   : 1847/03/25   Page: 042
Parents   : Sam And Sylva
Siblings : Crack, Manda and Infant 6 months old.
            Fanny was called "little" Fanny.

Name   : Ferdinand   Age : 22
Owner   : Snodgrass, Margaret And John
Year   : 1846/08/24   Page: 036
Wife   : Mariah,
Children : Monroe, Absalom, and Edny.

Name   : Flora   Age : 25
Owner   : Hamer, Amazon   And William H.
Year   : 1846/08/01   Page: 027
Note: Mulatto

Name   : Flora   Age : 70
Owner   : McIntyre, Emily   And Thomas G.
Year   : 1848/01/15   Page: 045

Name   : Fortune   Age : 2
Owner   : McIntyre, Emily   And Thomas G.
Year   : 1848/01/15   Page: 045

Name   : France   Age : 13
Owner   : Chambliss, Elizabeth And Cortez
Year   : 1847/10/13   Page: 063

Name   : Frank   Age : 7
Owner   : Davidson, Sarah   And Curvan
Year   : 1853/03/18   Page: 069
Mother   : Dela
Siblings : Jim and Martha.

PORT GIBSON PROPERTY LIST 1846-1858

Name   : Frank   Age : ?
Owner : Patton, Malinda   And Francis
Year   : 1846/06/26   Page: 006

Name   : Frank   Age : 10
Owner : Sayer, Harriet B. And William D.
Year   : 1847/03/03   Page: 041

Name   : Franklin   Age : ?
Owner : Patton, Malinda   And Francis
Year   : 1846/06/26   Page: 006

Name   : Franky   Age : 48
Owner : Buck, Maria   And William R.
Year   : 1846/08/27   Page: 038

Name   : Frederick   Age : ?
Owner : Mitchell, Harriet And John
Year   : 1857/09/22   Page: 061

Name   : Garland   Age : ?
Owner : Patton, Malinda   And Francis
Year   : 1846/06/26   Page: 006

Name   : George   Age : 12
Owner : Clarke, Martha   And Elijah L.
Year   : 1846/02/28   Page: 031
Note: George was the property of The
William Ervin Estate.

Name   : George   Age : 6
Owner : Gage, Rosanna   And James A.
Year   : 1846/07/20   Page: 016

Name   : George   Age : 13
Owner : McIntyre, Emily   And Thomas G.
Year   : 1848/01/15   Page: 045

Name   : George   Age : .6
Owner   : Snodgrass, Margaret And John
Year   : 1846/08/24   Page: 036
Mother : Harriet A.
Siblings: Conny.

PORT GIBSON PROPERTY
LIST 1846-1858

```
Name     : Gibson                          Age : 20
Owner    : Shaifer, Clarissa And Henry T.
Year     : 1852/06/24                      Page: 062

Name     : Gitty                           Age : 25
Owner    : Marye, Mary P.   And  James T.
Year     : 1846/08/18                      Page: 032

Name     : Goldsmith                       Age : 5
Owner    : Sillers, Caroline And William
Year     : 1846/02/08                      Page: 017
Parents  : Dick and Lucy
Siblings : Huldah and Louisa.

Name     : Grace                           Age : 6
Owner    : Magrunder, Sarah And Dr. Thomas B.
Year     : 1852/08/14                      Page: 067

Name     : Gracy                           Age : 5
Owner    : Coleman, Catharine And John
Year     : 1857/04/18                      Page: 061

Name     : Green                           Age : 10
Owner    : Spencer, Sarah A. And H. W.
Year     : 1846/02/28                      Page: 008
Mother   : Jane
Sibling  : Mike

Name     : Ham                             Age : ?
Owner    : Mitchell, Harriet And John
Year     : 1857/09/22                      Page: 061

Name     : Hamp                            Age : ?
Owner    : Bland, Emeline  And Maxwell W.
Year     : 1846/08/04                      Page: 024

Name     : Hampshire                       Age : 38
Owner    : Berry, Ellen A.  And Thomas
Year     : 1853/01/17                      Page: 068

Name     : Hankerson                       Age : ?
Owner    : Patton, Malinda And Francis
Year     : 1846/06/26                      Page: 006
```

PORT GIBSON PROPERTY
LIST 1846-1858

```
Name   : Hannah                       Age : 5
Owner  : Brown, Ann       And  Thomas W.
Year   : 1846/04/29                   Page: 001
Note: Ann Brown was heir of Ralph Regan.

Name   : Hardenia                     Age : 2
Owner  : Brown, Ann       And  Thomas W.
Year   : 1854/08/09                   Page: 076

Name   : Hariet                       Age : ?
Owner  : Brock, Vashti And Valentine W.
Year   : 1848/05/23                   Page: 048
Mother : Eliza
Sibling: Mariah, Matilda, Courtney, S? and
         Elizabeth.
Note: Vashti was heir of A. Brook from
Louisiana.

Name   : Haro                         Age : 28
Owner  : Brown, Ann       And  Thomas W.
Year   : 1846/04/29                   Page: 001
Note: Ann Brown was heir of Ralph Regan.

Name   : Harriet                      Age : 19
Owner  : Buck, Maria      And  William R.
Year   : 1846/08/27                   Page: 038

Name   : Harriet                      Age : 22
Owner  : McAlphine, Sally And William H.
Year   : 1854/01/01                   Page: 077
Note: Harriet was named "Little" Harriet.

Name   : Harriet                      Age : 30
Owner  : McAlphine, Sally And William H.
Year   : 1854/01/01                   Page: 077
Note: Harriet was named "Big" Harriet.

Name   : Harriet                      Age : 12
Owner  : Melchior, Sarah And John
Year   : 1846/08/21                   Page: 036

Name   : Harriet                      Age : 9
Owner  : Moore, Permelia And Rich M.
```

PORT GIBSON PROPERTY
LIST 1846-1858

Harriet(cont)
Year   : 1846/07/18   Page: 015
Note: Mulatto.

Name   : Harriet   Age : 20
Owner   : Snodgrass, Margaret And John
Year   : 1846/08/24   Page: 036
Children: Conny and George.

Name   : Harriet Ann   Age : 23
Owner   : Snodgrass, Margaret And John
Year   : 1846/08/24   Page: 036
Children: Clem, Chaney and Olevia.

Name   : Harriette   Age : 32
Owner   : McIntyre, Emily And Thomas G.
Year   : 1848/01/15   Page: 045

Name   : Harrison   Age : 45
Owner   : Griffins, Sarah And Francis
Year   : 1851/02/18   Page: 058

Name   : Harrison   Age : 22
Owner   : Rundell, Judith And Josiah Rundell
Year   : 1846/08/05   Page: 023

Name   : Harrison   Age : ?
Owner   : Shanahan, Elizabeth And Timothy
Year   : 1848/06/01   Page: 049
Note: Harrison was purchased in October 1843.

Name   : Harry   Age : 40
Owner   : Chambliss, Elizabeth And Cortez
Year   : 1847/10/13   Page: 063

Name   : Harve   Age : 8
Owner   : McIntyre, Emily And Thomas G.
Year   : 1848/01/15   Page: 045

Name   : Hector   Age : 45
Owner   : Sayer, Harriet B. And William D.
Year   : 1847/03/03   Page: 041

PORT GIBSON PROPERTY
LIST 1846-1858

```
Name   : Hector                          Age : 10
Owner  : Sayer, Harriet B. And William D.
Year   : 1847/03/03                      Page: 041

Name   : Henderson                       Age : 7
Owner  : Buck, Maria       And William R.
Year   : 1846/08/27                      Page: 038

Name   : Henderson                       Age : 17
Owner  : Clarke, Martha    And Elijah L.
Year   : 1846/02/28                      Page: 031

Name   : Henrietta                       Age : 22
Owner  : McAlphine, Sally And William H.
Year   : 1854/01/01                      Page: 077
Child  : Two month old infant.

Name   : Henry                           Age : 45
Owner  : Brock, Vashti And Valentine W.
Year   : 1848/05/23                      Page: 048
Note: Vashti was heir of A. Brook from
Louisiana.

Name   : Henry                           Age : 18
Owner  : Brown, Ann        And Thomas W.
Year   : 1846/04/29                      Page: 001
Note: Henry was related to Charity, Willis and
Jony. Ann Brown was heir of Ralph Regan.

Name   : Henry                           Age : 8
Owner  : Chambliss, Elizabeth And Cortez
Year   : 1847/10/13                      Page: 063

Name   : Henry                           Age : 29
Owner  : Clarke, Martha    And Elijah L.
Year   : 1846/02/28                      Page: 031
Note: Henry was the property of The
William Ervin Estate.

Name   : Henry                           Age : 16
Owner  : McAlphine, Sally And William H.
Year   : 1854/01/01                      Page: 077
```

PORT GIBSON PROPERTY
LIST 1846-1858

```
Name     : Henry                    Age : 6
Owner    : McGilvary, Mary And Alexander
Year     : 1846/08/18               Page: 030
Mother   : Caroline
Siblings : Charles and Lucy.

Name     : Henry                    Age : 8
Owner    : McIntyre, Emily And Thomas G.
Year     : 1848/01/15               Page: 045

Name     : Henry                    Age : 27
Owner    : McIntyre, Emily And Thomas G.
Year     : 1848/01/15               Page: 045

Name     : Henry                    Age : ?
Owner    : Patton, Malinda And Francis
Year     : 1846/06/26               Page: 006

Name     : Henry                    Age : 23
Owner    : Shaifer, Elizabeth And Abram K.
Year     : 1846/06/10               Page: 003

Name     : Henson                   Age : 35
Owner    : Thomson, Elizabeth And Thomas W.
Year     : 1846/07/02               Page: 013

Name     : Hester                   Age : 8
Owner    : McIntyre, Emily And Thomas G.
Year     : 1848/01/15               Page: 045

Name     : Hester                   Age : ?
Owner    : Mitchell, Harriet And John
Year     : 1857/09/22               Page: 061

Name     : Hester                   Age : 7
Owner    : Sillers, Caroline And William
Year     : 1846/07/22               Page: 018
Mother   : Cely
Siblings : Wash, Ebb, Park, Mary, Betsy and
           Amos.

Name     : Hetta                    Age : 70
Owner    : McIntyre, Emily And Thomas G.
```

PORT GIBSON PROPERTY
LIST 1846-1858

Hetta(cont)
Year   : 1848/01/15   Page: 045

Name   : Hinds   Age : 23
Owner   : Brown, Ann   And   Thomas W.
Year   : 1854/08/09   Page: 076

Name   : Horace   Age : 4
Owner   : Buck, Maria   And   William R.
Year   : 1846/08/27   Page: 038

Name   : Huldah   Age : 4
Owner   : Sillers, Caroline And William
Year   : 1846/02/08   Page: 017
Parents : Dick and Lucy.
Siblings : Goldsmith and Louise.

Name   : Humphreys   Age : ?
Owner   : Stamps, Jane And   Volney
Year   : 1846/08/03   Page: 021
Mother   : Eliza
Sibling : Junius, Crockett, Irene,
           Albert, Victoria and Ina.

Name   : Ike   Age : 46
Owner   : McIntyre, Emily And   Thomas G.
Year   : 1848/01/15   Page: 045

Name   : Ike   Age : 6
Owner   : McIntyre, Emily And   Thomas G.
Year   : 1848/01/15   Page: 045

Name   : Ina   Age : ?
Owner   : Stamps, Jane And   Volney
Year   : 1846/08/03   Page: 021
Mother   : Eliza
Sibling : Junius, Crockett, Humphreys and
           Victoria.

Name   : Indiana   Age : 4
Owner   : Shaifer, Clarissa And Henry T.
Year   : 1852/06/24   Page: 062

PORT GIBSON PROPERTY
LIST 1846-1858

```
Name     : Infant                      Age : .6
Owner    : Sims, Emeline F. And Isaac A.
Year     : 1847/03/25                  Page: 042
Parents  : Sam and Sylva.
Siblings : Little Fanny, Crack and Manda.

Name     : Irene                       Age : ?
Owner    : Stamps, Jane    And Volney
Year     : 1846/08/03                  Page: 021
Mother   : Eliza
Siblings : Junius, Crockett, Humphreys, Albert,
           Victoria and Ina.

Name     : Isaac                       Age : ?
Owner    : Bland, Emeline  And Maxwell W.
Year     : 1846/08/04                  Page: 024

Name     : Isaac                       Age : 20
Owner    : Chambliss, Mary And Calvin
Year     : 1858/12/10                  Page: 081

Name     : Isaac                       Age : 14
Owner    : McAlphine, Sally And William H.
Year     : 1854/01/01                  Page: 077

Name     : Isaac                       Age : 50
Owner    : Sayer, Harriet B. And William D.
Year     : 1847/03/03                  Page: 041

Name     : Isabel                      Age : 18
Owner    : Shaifer, Clarissa And Henry T.
Year     : 1852/06/24                  Page: 062

Name     : Isham                       Age : ?
Owner    : Patton, Malinda And Francis
Year     : 1846/06/26                  Page: 006

Name     : Isham                       Age : 50
Owner    : Posey, Sarah    And Humphrey M.
Year     : 1846/07/04                  Page: 007

Name     : Isham                       Age : 26
Owner    : Shaifer, Elizabeth And Abram K.
```

PORT GIBSON PROPERTY
LIST 1846-1858

Isham(cont)
Year   : 1846/06/10   Page: 003

Name   : Jack   Age : ?
Owner   : Bland, Emeline   And Maxwell W.
Year   : 1846/08/04   Page: 024

Name   : Jack   Age : 20
Owner   : Brown, Ann   And Thomas W.
Year   : 1854/08/09   Page: 076

Name   : Jack   Age : 24
Owner   : Clarke, Martha   And Elijah L.
Year   : 1846/02/28   Page: 031
Note: Jack was the property of The
William Ervin Estate.

Name   : Jack   Age : 10
Owner   : Gage, Rosanna   And James A.
Year   : 1846/07/20   Page: 016

Name   : Jack   Age : 55
Owner   : Hamer, Amazon   And William H.
Year   : 1846/08/01   Page: 027
Note: Jack was born in Africa.

Name   : Jack   Age : ?
Owner   : Merrill, Caroline And A. P.
Year   : 1848/05/04   Page: 046

Name   : Jack   Age : ?
Owner   : Mitchell, Harriet And John
Year   : 1857/09/22   Page: 061

Name   : Jack   Age : ?
Owner   : Rossman, Hariet And Dr. Walter
Year   : 1846/07/21   Page: 017

Name   : Jack   Age : 1
Owner   : Sayer, Harriet B. And William D.
Year   : 1847/03/03   Page: 041

Name   : Jack   Age : 26

PORT GIBSON PROPERTY
LIST 1846-1858

Jack(cont)
Owner : Snodgrass, Margaret And John
Year : 1846/08/24   Page: 036

Name : Jack Stevenson   Age : 28
Owner : Wilson, Elizabeth And Charles W.
Year : 1846/07/31   Page: 019

Name : Jacks   Age : 40
Owner : McAlphine, Sally And William H.
Year : 1854/01/01   Page: 077

Name : Jackson   Age : 25
Owner : McAlphine, Harriet And William H.
Year : 1854/12/01   Page:

Name : Jackson   Age : 3
Owner : Shaifer, Clarissa And Henry T.
Year : 1852/06/24   Page: 062

Name : Jake   Age : 24
Owner : Brown, Ann   And Thomas W.
Year : 1846/04/29   Page: 001
Note: Jake was related to Mary, Jesse, and Little Charles. Ann Brown was heir of Ralph Regan.

Name : Jake   Age : 35
Owner : Buck, Maria   And William R.
Year : 1846/08/27   Page: 038

Name : Jane   Age : 37
Owner : Brock, Vashti And Valentine W.
Year : 1848/05/23   Page: 048
Note: Vashti was heir of A. Brook from Louisiana.
Child : Charles.

Name : Jane   Age : 10
Owner : Brock, Vashti And Valentine W.
Year : 1848/05/23   Page: 048
Note: Vashti was heir of A. Brook from Louisiana. Jane was an orphan.

PORT GIBSON PROPERTY
LIST 1846-1858

```
Name     : Jane                         Age : 9
Owner    : McIntyre, Emily  And  Thomas G.
Year     : 1848/01/15                   Page: 045

Name     : Jane                         Age : ?
Owner    : Mitchell, Harriet And  John
Year     : 1857/09/22                   Page: 061

Name     : Jane                         Age : 3
Owner    : Patterson, Louise And  James H.
Year     : 1854/05/02                   Page: 074
Mother   : Betsy
Sibling  : Julia.

Name     : Jane                         Age : 11
Owner    : Shaifer, Clarissa And  Henry T.
Year     : 1852/06/24                   Page: 062

Name     : Jane                         Age : 35
Owner    : Spencer, Sarah A. And  H. W.
Year     : 1846/02/28                   Page: 008
Children : Green and Mike.

Name     : Jeff                         Age : 16
Owner    : Chambliss, Elizabeth And  Cortez
Year     : 1847/10/13                   Page: 063

Name     : Jeff                         Age : 26
Owner    : Sims, Emeline F. And  Isaac A.
Year     : 1847/03/25                   Page: 042

Name     : Jefferson                    Age : 45
Owner    : McIntyre, Emily  And  Thomas G.
Year     : 1848/01/15                   Page: 044

Name     : Jeffrey                      Age : ?
Owner    : Bland, Emeline  And  Maxwell W.
Year     : 1846/03/08                   Page: 041

Name     : Jeffrey                      Age : 40
Owner    : Snodgrass, Margaret And  John
Year     : 1846/08/24                   Page: 036
```

PORT GIBSON PROPERTY
LIST 1846-1858

Name   : Jeffrey   Age : 29
Owner   : Spencer, Sarah A. And H. W.
Year   : 1846/02/28   Page: 008

Name   : Jeffrey   Age : 1
Owner   : Spencer, Sarah A. And H. W.
Year   : 1846/02/28   Page: 008
Mother   : Cynthia
Siblings: Ellen, Cora, Aruelia and Priscialla.

Name   : Jenny   Age : 17
Owner   : Spencer, Sarah A. And H. W.
Year   : 1846/02/28   Page: 008

Name   : Jerry   Age : ?
Owner   : Bland, Emeline   And   Maxwell W.
Year   : 1846/08/04   Page: 024

Name   : Jerry   Age : 35
Owner   : Coleman, Catharine And John
Year   : 1857/04/18   Page: 061

Name   : Jerry   Age : 4
Owner   : McIntyre, Emily   And   Thomas G.
Year   : 1848/01/15   Page: 045

Name   : Jerry   Age : ?
Owner   : Mitchell, Harriet And John
Year   : 1857/09/22   Page: 061

Name   : Jerry   Age : ?
Owner   : Patton, Malinda And   Francis
Year   : 1846/06/26   Page: 006

Name   : Jerry   Age : 15
Owner   : Snodgrass, Margaret And John
Year   : 1846/08/24   Page: 036

Name   : Jerry   Age : 20
Owner   : Thomson, Elizabeth And Thomas W.
Year   : 1846/07/02   Page: 013

Name   : Jesse   Age : 13

PORT GIBSON PROPERTY
LIST 1846-1858

Jesse(cont)
Owner : Brown, Ann   And Thomas W.
Year : 1846/04/29   Page: 001
Note: Jesse was related to Jake, Mary and
Charles. Ann Brown was heir of Ralph Regan.

Name : Jesse   Age : 28
Owner : Griffins, Sarah And Francis
Year : 1850/07/08   Page: 057

Name : Jim   Age : 15
Owner : Berry, Ellen A. And Thomas
Year : 1853/01/17   Page: 068

Name : Jim   Age : 28
Owner : Buck, Maria   And William R.
Year : 1846/08/27   Page: 038

Name : Jim   Age : 45
Owner : Clarke, Martha   And Elijah L.
Year : 1846/02/28   Page: 031
Note: Jim was the property of the William Ervin
Estate.

Name : Jim   Age : 31
Owner : Clarke, Martha   And Elijah L.
Year : 1846/02/28   Page: 031
Note:Jim was the property of the William Ervin
Estate.

Name   : Jim   Age : 3
Owner   : Davidson, Sarah And Curvan
Year   : 1853/03/18   Page: 069
Mother : Dela
Siblings: Frank and Martha.

Name : Jim   Age : 14
Owner : Griffins, Sarah And Francis
Year : 1850/07/08   Page: 057

Name : Jim   Age : 27
Owner : McAlphine, Sally And William H.
Year : 1854/01/01   Page: 077

PORT GIBSON PROPERTY
LIST 1846-1858

Name : Jim   Age : 35
Owner : McDougall, Elizabeth And Nicholas
Year : 1846/08/13   Page: 025

Name : Jim   Age : 30
Owner : McDougall, Susan And Daniel
Year : 1846/06/30   Page: 020

Name : Jim   Age : 36
Owner : McDougall, Susan And Daniel
Year : 1853/02/02   Page: 070

Name : Jim   Age : 60
Owner : McIntyre, Emily And Thomas G.
Year : 1848/01/15   Page: 045

Name : Jim   Age : 14
Owner : McIntyre, Emily And Thomas G.
Year : 1848/01/15   Page: 045

Name : Jim   Age : ?
Owner : Patton, Malinda And Francis
Year : 1846/06/26   Page: 006

Name : Jinny   Age : 26
Owner : Gage, Rosanna And James A.
Year : 1846/07/20   Page: 016

Name : Joe   Age : ?
Owner : Bland, Emeline And Maxwell W.
Year : 1846/08/04   Page: 024

Name : Joe   Age : 6
Owner : Clarke, Martha And Elijah L.
Year : 1846/02/28   Page: 031
Note: Joe was the property of The William Ervin Estate.

Name : Joe   Age : 26
Owner : McIntyre, Emily And Thomas G.
Year : 1848/01/15   Page: 045

Name : Joe   Age : ?

PORT GIBSON PROPERTY
LIST 1846-1858

```
Joe(cont)
Owner   : Patton, Malinda And Francis
Year    : 1846/06/26            Page: 006

Name    : Joe                   Age : ?
Owner   : Patton, Malinda And Francis
Year    : 1846/06/26            Page: 006

Name    : Joe                   Age : 25
Owner   : Spencer, Sarah A. And H. W.
Year    : 1846/02/28            Page: 008

Name    : Joe                   Age : 9
Owner   : Thomson, Caroline And Benjamin W.
Year    : 1846/08/04            Page: 041
Parents : Buck And Emily.
Sibling : Andrew, Alice and Mary.

Name    : John                  Age : 30
Owner   : Buck, Maria     And William R.
Year    : 1846/08/27            Page: 038

Name    : John                  Age : 6
Owner   : Frisby, Elizabeth And Aaron
Year    : 1846/07/03            Page: 010

Name    : John                  Age : 18
Owner   : Hamer, Amazon   And William H.
Year    : 1846/08/01            Page: 027

Name    : John                  Age : 48
Owner   : Marye, Mary P.  And James T.
Year    : 1848/05/06            Page: 048

Name    : John                  Age : 5
Owner   : McIntyre, Emily And Thomas G.
Year    : 1848/01/15            Page: 045

Name    : John                  Age : 25
Owner   : Robinson, Mary  And James H.
Year    : 1846/07/26            Page: 028

Name    : John                  Age : 21
```

PORT GIBSON PROPERTY
LIST 1846-1858

John(cont)
Owner : Sillers, Caroline And William
Year : 1846/07/22   Page: 018

Name : Jordan   Age : 8
Owner : Brown, Ann   And Thomas W.
Year : 1846/04/29   Page: 001
Note: Ann Brown was heir of Ralph Regan.

Name : Jordan   Age : 22
Owner : Chambliss, Elizabeth And Cortez
Year : 1847/10/13   Page: 063

Name   : Joseph   Age : .9
Owner   : Sillers, Caroline And William
Year   : 1846/07/22   Page: 018
Parents : Bill and Mary Ann.
Siblings: Martha, Van Buren and Ralph Jr.

Name   : Josephine   Age : 3
Owner   : Brock, Vashti And Valentine W.
Year   : 1848/05/23   Page: 048
Mother : Milly
Sibling : Elizabeth
Note: Vashti was heir of A. Brook from Louisiana.

Name : Josh   Age : 17
Owner : McIntyre, Emily And Thomas G.
Year : 1848/01/15   Page: 045

Name : Judy   Age : .5
Owner : Brown, Ann   And Thomas W.
Year : 1846/04/29   Page: 001
Note: Ann Brown was heir of Ralph Regan.

Name : Julia   Age : 25
Owner : Frisby, Elizabeth And Aaron
Year : 1846/07/03   Page: 010

Name : Julia   Age : ?
Owner : Mitchell, Harriet And John
Year : 1857/09/22   Page: 061

PORT GIBSON PROPERTY
LIST 1846-1858

Name   : Julia   Age : 3
Owner   : Patterson, Louise And James H.
Year   : 1854/05/02   Page: 074
Mother : Betsy
Sibling : Jane

Name   : Julian   Age : 3
Owner   : Buck, Maria   And William R.
Year   : 1846/08/27   Page: 038

Name   : Junius   Age : ?
Owner   : Stamps, Jane   And Volney
Year   : 1846/08/03   Page: 021
Mother : Eliza
Siblings: Crockett, Humphreys, Irene, Albert, Victoria and Ina.

Name   : Kate   Age : ?
Owner   : Stamps, Jane   And Volney
Year   : 1846/08/03   Page: 021
Mother : Sarah
Sibling : Billy

Name   : Kentuck   Age : ?
Owner   : Patton, Malinda And Francis
Year   : 1846/06/26   Page: 006

Name   : Kitty   Age : 23
Owner   : Coleman, Catharine And John
Year   : 1857/04/18   Page: 061

Name   : Larkin   Age : 3
Owner   : Wilson, Elizabeth And Charles W.
Year   : 1846/07/31   Page: 019

Name   : Laura   Age : 3
Owner   : Coleman, Catharine And John
Year   : 1857/04/18   Page: 061

Name   : Laura   Age : 40
Owner   : Wilson, Elizabeth And Charles W.
Year   : 1846/07/31   Page: 019

PORT GIBSON PROPERTY
LIST 1846-1858

Name : Lavine   Age : 3
Owner : McIntyre, Emily And Thomas G.
Year : 1848/01/15   Page: 045

Name : Lavinia   Age : 1
Owner : McIntyre, Emily And Thomas G.
Year : 1848/01/15   Page: 045

Name : Leonard   Age : 17
Owner : Snodgrass, Margaret And John
Year : 1846/08/24   Page: 036

Name : Lethe   Age : .4
Owner : McIntyre, Emily And Thomas G.
Year : 1848/01/15   Page: 045

Name : Levi   Age : 18
Owner : Clarke, Martha   And Elijah L.
Year : 1846/02/28   Page: 031
Note: Levi was the property of the William Ervin Estate.

Name : Lewis   Age : ?
Owner : Bland, Emeline   And Maxwell W.
Year : 1846/08/04   Page: 024

Name : Lewis   Age : 1
Owner : Marye, Mary P.   And James T.
Year : 1846/08/18   Page: 032

Name : Lewis   Age : 19
Owner : Robinson, Mary   And James H.
Year : 1846/07/26   Page: 028

Name : Lewis   Age : 27
Owner : St. John, Ellen And John H.
Year : 1846/01/27   Page: 039

Name : Lexy   Age : 9
Owner : McIntyre, Emily And Thomas G.
Year : 1848/01/15   Page: 045

Name : Littleton   Age : 23

PORT GIBSON PROPERTY
LIST 1846-1858

Littleton(cont)
Owner : McIntyre, Emily And Thomas G.
Year : 1848/01/15   Page: 045

Name : Lively   Age : 11
Owner : Brown, Ann   And Thomas W.
Year : 1854/08/09   Page: 076

Name : Logan   Age : ?
Owner : Patton, Malinda And Francis
Year : 1846/06/26   Page: 006

Name : Lorinda   Age : 13
Owner : Buck, Maria   And William R.
Year : 1846/08/27   Page: 038

Name : Louis   Age : 40
Owner : Chambliss, Eliza And Cortez
Year : 1847/10/13   Page: 063

Name : Louisa   Age : 25
Owner : McAlphine, Sally And William H.
Year : 1854/01/01   Page: 077

Name : Louisa   Age : 30
Owner : McIntyre, Emily And Thomas G.
Year : 1848/01/15   Page: 045

Name : Louisa   Age : ?
Owner : Rundell, Judith And Josiah Rundell
Year : 1846/08/05   Page: 024
Child : Paris

Name : Louisa   Age : 18
Owner : Rundell, Judith And William H.
Year : 1846/08/05   Page:

Name   : Louise   Age : 6
Owner   : Brock, Vashti And Valentine W.
Year   : 1848/05/23   Page: 048
Mother : Lucinda
Sibling : Allis
Note: Vashti was heir of A. Brook from La.

96

PORT GIBSON PROPERTY
LIST 1846-1858

Name   : Louise   Age : 10
Owner   : Sillers, Caroline And William
Year   : 1846/02/08   Page: 017
Parents : Dick and Lucy.
Sibling : Goldsmith, Huldah and Louisa.

Name   : Lucinda   Age : 30
Owner   : Brock, Vashti And Valentine W.
Year   : 1848/05/23   Page: 048
Children: Louise and Allis.
Note: Vashti was heir of A. Brook from Louisiana.

Name   : Lucinda   Age : ?
Owner   : Merrill, Caroline And A. P.
Year   : 1848/05/04   Page: 046

Name   : Lucy   Age : 25
Owner   : Brown, Ann   And Thomas W.
Year   : 1846/04/29   Page: 001
Note: Ann Brown was heir of Ralph Regan.

Name   : Lucy   Age : 16
Owner   : Clarke, Martha   And Elijah L.
Year   : 1846/02/28   Page: 031
Child   : William
Note:Lucy was the property of The William Ervin Estate.

Name   : Lucy   Age : 32
Owner   : Magrunder, Sarah And Dr. Thomas B.
Year   : 1852/08/14   Page: 067

Name   : Lucy   Age : .20
Owner   : McDougall, Susan And Daniel
Year   : 1853/02/02   Page: 070
Mother : Sarah
Sibling : Elsey
Note: Mulatto

Name   : Lucy   Age : 3
Owner   : McGilvary, Mary And Alexander
Year   : 1846/08/18   Page: 030

PORT GIBSON PROPERTY LIST 1846-1858

Lucy(cont)
Mother : Caroline
Sibling : Charles and Henry.

Name   : Lucy   Age : 28
Owner : Rivers, Mary W. And Orville C.
Year   : 1851/04/10   Page: 058

Name   : Lucy   Age : 5
Owner : Sayer, Harriet B. And William D.
Year   : 1847/03/03   Page: 041

Name   : Lucy   Age : 19
Owner : Shaifer, Clarissa And Henry T.
Year   : 1852/06/24   Page: 062

Name   : Lucy   Age : 25
Owner   : Sillers, Caroline And William
Year   : 1846/02/08   Page: 017
Husband : Dick
Children : GoldSmith, Huldah, and Louise.

Name   : Lucy   Age : 33
Owner : Spencer, Sarah A. And H. W.
Year   : 1846/02/28   Page: 008

Name   : M   Age : ?
Owner : Patton, Malinda And Francis
Year   : 1846/06/26   Page: 006

Name   : Maborn   Age : 16
Owner : Brown, Ann   And Thomas W.
Year   : 1846/04/29   Page: 001
Note: Ann Brown was heir of Ralph Regan.

Name   : Magaret   Age : 14
Owner : Hamer, Amazon   And Willam H.
Year   : 1846/08/01   Page: 027
Note: Mulatto.

Name   : Malinda   Age : 40
Owner : Brown, Ann   And Thomas W.
Year   : 1854/08/09   Page: 076

PORT GIBSON PROPERTY LIST 1846-1858

```
Name      : Malinda                        Age : ?
Owner     : Chambliss, Mary  And  Calvin T.
Year      : 1852/08/09                     Page: 066

Name      : Manda                          Age : 3
Owner     : Sims, Emeline F.  And  Isaac A.
Year      : 1847/03/25                     Page: 042
Parent    : Sam and Sylva
Siblings  : Little Fanny, Crack and Infant
            6 months old.

Name      : Manerva                        Age : 6
Owner     : McIntyre, Emily  And  Thomas G.
Year      : 1848/01/15                     Page: 045

Name      : Manson                         Age : 8
Owner     : Magrunder, Sarah  And  Dr. Thomas B.
Year      : 1852/08/14                     Page: 067

Name      : Manuel                         Age : 15
Owner     : Chambliss, Elizabeth  And  Cortez
Year      : 1847/10/13                     Page: 063
Name      : March                          Age : 11

Owner     : McIntyre, Emily  And  Thomas G.
Year      : 1848/01/15                     Page: 045
Name      : Margaret                       Age : 24

Owner     : McIntyre, Emily  And  Thomas G.
Year      : 1848/01/15                     Page: 044
Name      : Marge                          Age : ?

Owner     : Patton, Malinda  And  Francis
Year      : 1846/06/26                     Page: 006
Name      : Maria                          Age : 25

Owner     : Coleman, Catharine  And  John
Year      : 1857/04/18                     Page: 061

Name      : Maria                          Age : 40
Owner     : Forbes, Sarah Ann  And  Spooner
Year      : 1846/08/14                     Page: 026
```

PORT GIBSON PROPERTY LIST 1846-1858

Name   : Maria   Age : 28
Owner : Marye, Mary P.   And James T.
Year   : 1846/08/18   Page: 032

Name   : Mariah   Age : ?
Owner   : Brock, Vashti And Valentine W.
Year   : 1848/05/23   Page: 048
Mother : Eliza
Sibling : Matilda, Courtney, Hariet, Sam,
          Chapurner and Elizabeth.
Note: Vashti Was Heir Of A. Brook From Louisiana.

Name   : Mariah   Age : 35
Owner : McIntyre, Emily And Thomas G.
Year   : 1848/01/15   Page: 045

Name   : Mariah   Age : 20
Owner   : Snodgrass, Margaret And John
Year   : 1846/08/24   Page: 036
Husband : Ferdinand
Children : Monroe, Absalom and Edny.

Name   : Mark   Age : .4
Owner : Brown, Ann   And Thomas W.
Year   : 1846/04/29   Page: 001
Note: Ann Brown was heir of Ralph Regan.

Name   : Marmaduke   Age : 7
Owner : McIntyre, Emily And Thomas G.
Year   : 1848/01/15   Page: 045

Name   : Martha   Age : 7
Owner : Brown, Ann   And Thomas W.
Year   : 1846/04/29   Page: 001
Note: Ann Brown was heir of Ralph Regan.

Name   : Martha   Age : 5
Owner   : Davidson, Sarah And Curvan
Year   : 1853/03/18   Page: 069
Mother : Dela
Sibling : Frank and Jim.

PORT GIBSON PROPERTY
LIST 1846-1858

Name   : Martha   Age : 12
Owner   : Hamer, Amazon   And William H.
Year   : 1846/08/01   Page: 027

Name   : Martha   Age : ?
Owner   : Mitchell, Harriet And John
Year   : 1857/09/22   Page: 061

Name   : Martha   Age : ?
Owner   : Patton, Malinda And Francis
Year   : 1846/06/26   Page: 006

Name   : Martha   Age : 27
Owner   : Porter, Elizabeth And D. R.
Year   : 1854/05/24   Page: 075
Children: Matilda and Charolotte.
Note: Martha was purchased from T.F. Lindsey On January 4, 1851.

Name   : Martha   Age : 14
Owner   : Shaifer, Clarissa And Henry T.
Year   : 1852/06/24   Page: 062

Name   : Martha   Age : 17
Owner   : Sillers, Caroline And William
Year   : 1846/07/22   Page: 018
Mother : Mary Ann
Siblings: Van Buren, Ralph Jr. and Joseph.

Name   : Martha   Age : 15
Owner   : Thomson, Elizabeth And Thomas W.
Year   : 1846/07/02   Page: 013

Name   : Mary   Age : 17
Owner   : Brown, Ann   And Thomas W.
Year   : 1846/04/29   Page: 001
Note: Mary was related to Jake, Jesse and Little Charles. Ann Brown was heir Of Ralph Regan.

Name   : Mary   Age : 20
Owner   : Hamer, Amazon   And William H.
Year   : 1846/08/01   Page: 027

PORT GIBSON PROPERTY
LIST 1846-1858

Name : Mary   Age : 4
Owner : McDougall, Ann E. And Duncan
Year : 1846/07/02   Page: 006

Name : Mary   Age : 26
Owner : McDougall, Susan And Daniel
Year : 1846/07/30   Page: 020

Name : Mary   Age : 19
Owner : McDougall, Susan And Daniel
Year : 1853/02/02   Page: 070

Name : Mary   Age : 28
Owner : McIntyre, Emily And Thomas G.
Year : 1848/01/15   Page: 045

Name : Mary   Age : ?
Owner : Mitchell, Harriet And John
Year : 1857/09/22   Page: 061

Name : Mary   Age : ?
Owner : Patton, Malinda And Francis
Year : 1846/06/26   Page: 006
Note: Mary was called "Big" Mary.

Name : Mary   Age : ?
Owner : Patton, Malinda And Francis
Year : 1846/06/26   Page: 006
Note: Mary was called "Little" Mary.

Name : Mary   Age : ?
Owner : Patton, Malinda And Francis
Year : 1846/06/26   Page: 006

Name   : Mary   Age : 4
Owner   : Rivers, Mary W. And Orville C.
Year   : 1851/04/10   Page: 058
Mother   : Lucy
Siblings : Catharine and Eliza.

Name : Mary   Age : 30
Owner : Robinson, Mary And James H.
Year : 1846/07/26   Page: 028

PORT GIBSON PROPERTY LIST 1846-1858

```
Name    : Mary                          Age : ?
Owner   : Rossman, Hariet  And  Dr. Walter
Year    : 1846/07/21                    Page: 017

Name    : Mary                          Age : 17
Owner   : Sayer, Harriet B. And  William D.
Year    : 1847/03/03                    Page: 041
Child   : Ned

Name    : Mary                          Age : 4
Owner   : Sayer, Harriet B. And  William D.
Year    : 1847/03/03                    Page: 041

Name    : Mary                          Age : 18
Owner   : Sayer, Harriet B. And  William D.
Year    : 1847/03/03                    Page: 041

Name    : Mary                          Age : 40
Owner   : Shaifer, Elizabeth And  Abram K.
Year    : 1846/06/10                    Page: 003
Husband : William
Children: Cyrus, Suzette, Amerricus and Mary
          Ann.

Name    : Mary                          Age : 11
Owner   : Sillers, Caroline And  William
Year    : 1846/07/22                    Page: 018
Mother  : Cely
Siblings: Wash, Ebb, Park, Betsy, Hester,
          and Amos.

Name    : Mary                          Age : 22
Owner   : St. John, Ellen  And  John H.
Year    : 1846/01/27                    Page: 039

Name    : Mary                          Age : .10
Owner   : Thomson, Caroline And  Benjamin W.
Year    : 1846/08/04                    Page: 041
Parents : Buck and Emily
Siblings: Joe, Andrew and Alice.

Name    : Mary Ann                      Age : 1
Owner   : Shaifer, Elizabeth And  Abram K.
```

PORT GIBSON PROPERTY
LIST 1846-1858

Mary Ann(cont)
Year   : 1846/06/10   Page: 003
Parents : William and Mary
Siblings : Cyrus, Suzette and Amerricus.

Name   : Mary Ann   Age : 37
Owner   : Sillers, Caroline And William
Year   : 1846/07/22   Page: 018
Husband : Bill
Children : Martha, Van Buren, Ralph Jr, and
           Joseph.

Name   : Mary Jane   Age : 1
Owner   : Coleman, Catharine And John
Year   : 1857/04/18   Page: 061

Name   : Matilda   Age : ?
Owner   : Brock, Vashti And Valentine W.
Year   : 1848/05/23   Page: 048
Mother   : Eliza
Siblings : Mariah, Courtney, Hariet, Sam,
           Chapurnur, and Elizabeth.
Note: Vashti was heir of A. Brook from
Louisiana.

Name   : Matilda   Age : 8
Owner   : Buck, Maria And William R.
Year   : 1846/08/27   Page: 038

Name   : Matilda   Age : 17
Owner   : Coleman, Catharine And John
Year   : 1857/04/18   Page: 061

Name   : Matilda   Age : 4
Owner   : Porter, Elizabeth And D. R.?
Year   : 1854/05/24   Page: 075
Mother   : Martha
Sibling : Charolotte
Note: Purchased from T.F. Lindsey on January 4,
1851.

Name   : Mike   Age : ?
Owner   : Mitchell, Harriet and John.

PORT GIBSON PROPERTY
LIST 1846-1858

Mike(cont)
Year   : 1857/09/22   Page: 061

Name   : Mike   Age : 35
Owner   : Sayer, Harriet B. And William D.
Year   : 1847/03/03   Page: 041

Name   : Mike   Age : 8
Owner   : Spencer, Sarah A. And H. W.
Year   : 1846/02/28   Page: 008
Mother : Jane
Sibling : Green

Name   : Miles   Age : ?
Owner   : Patton, Malinda And Francis
Year   : 1846/06/26   Page: 006

Name   : Milly   Age : ?
Owner   : Bland, Emeline And Maxwell W.
Year   : 1846/08/04   Page: 024

Name   : Milly   Age : ?
Owner   : Mitchell, Harriet And John
Year   : 1857/09/22   Page: 061

Name   : Milly   Age : 40
Owner   : Thomson, Caroline And Benjamin W.
Year   : 1851/02/12   Page: 056
Child   : Dennis.

Name   : Mima   Age : 8
Owner   : Frisby, Elizabeth And Aaron
Year   : 1846/07/03   Page: 010

Name   : Minerva   Age : 12
Owner   : Griffins, Sarah And Francis
Year   : 1850/07/08   Page: 057
Note: Minerva was purchased from Isaac D. Adams.

Name   : Minerva   Age : 8
Owner   : Sayer, Harriet B. And William D.
Year   : 1847/03/03   Page: 041

PORT GIBSON PROPERTY LIST 1846-1858

```
Name   : Mira                        Age : 8
Owner  : Brown, Ann        And  Thomas W.
Year   : 1846/04/29                  Page: 001
Note: Mira was related to Rachel, Moses and
Nancy. Ann Brown was heir of Ralph Regan.

Name   : Missouri                    Age : 10
Owner  : McIntyre, Emily   And  Thomas G.
Year   : 1848/01/15                  Page: 045

Name   : Missouri                    Age : 26
Owner  : Rundell, Judith   And  Josiah Rundell
Year   : 1846/08/05                  Page: 023

Name   : Monk                        Age : 32
Owner  : Sims, Emeline F.  And  Isaac A.
Year   : 1847/03/25                  Page: 042
Wife   : Fanny

Name   : Monroe                      Age : 4
Owner  : Snodgrass, Margaret And  John
Year   : 1846/08/24                  Page: 036
Parents : Ferdinand and Mariah
Siblings: Absalom and Edny.

Name   : Monroe                      Age : 18
Owner  : Snodgrass, Margaret And  John
Year   : 1846/08/24                  Page: 036

Name   : Mose                        Age : 45
Owner  : Buck, Maria       And  William R.
Year   : 1846/08/27                  Page: 038

Name   : Moses                       Age : 35
Owner  : Brown, Ann        And  Thomas W.
Year   : 1846/04/29                  Page: 001
Note: Moses was related to Rachel, Mira And
Nancy. Ann Brown was heir of Ralph Regan.

Name   : Moses                       Age : 19
Owner  : Coleman, Catharine And  John
Year   : 1857/04/18                  Page: 061
```

PORT GIBSON PROPERTY LIST 1846-1858

```
Name   : Moses                      Age : 32
Owner  : Hamer, Amazon    And  William H.
Year   : 1846/08/01                 Page: 027

Name   : Mourning                   Age : 9
Owner  : Brown, Ann       And  Thomas W.
Year   : 1846/04/29                 Page: 001
Note: Ann Brown was heir of Ralph Regan.

Name   : Myra                       Age : 25
Owner  : Hamer, Amazon    And  William H.
Year   : 1846/08/01                 Page: 027

Name   : Nancy                      Age : ?
Owner  : Bland, Emeline   And  Maxwell W.
Year   : 1846/08/04                 Page: 024

Name   : Nancy                      Age : 6
Owner  : Brown, Ann       And  Thomas W.
Year   : 1846/04/29                 Page: 001
Note: Nancy was related to Rachel, Moses and
Mira. Ann Brown was heir of Ralph Regan.

Name   : Nancy                      Age : 30
Owner  : Coleman, Catharine And  John
Year   : 1857/04/18                 Page: 061

Name   : Nancy                      Age : 65
Owner  : McIntyre, Emily  And  Thomas G.
Year   : 1848/01/15                 Page: 045

Name   : Nancy                      Age : ?
Owner  : Mitchell, Harriet And  John
Year   : 1857/09/22                 Page: 061

Name   : Nancy                      Age : ?
Owner  : Patton, Malinda  And  Francis
Year   : 1846/06/26                 Page: 006

Name   : Ned                        Age : ?
Owner  : Bland, Emeline   And  Maxwell W.
Year   : 1846/03/08                 Page: 041
```

PORT GIBSON PROPERTY
LIST 1846-1858

Name   : Ned   Age : ?
Owner : Bland, Emeline   And   Maxwell W.
Year   : 1846/08/04   Page: 024
Mother : Louisa

Name   : Ned   Age : 32
Owner : Brown, Ann   And   Thomas W.
Year   : 1846/04/29   Page: 001
Note: Ann Brown was heir of Ralph Regan.

Name   : Ned   Age : 38
Owner : Marye, Mary P.   And   James T.
Year   : 1846/08/18   Page: 032

Name   : Ned   Age : 45
Owner : Sayer, Harriet B. And   William D.
Year   : 1847/03/03   Page: 041

Name   : Ned   Age : .1
Owner : Sayer, Harriet B. And   William D.
Year   : 1847/03/03   Page: 041
Mother : Mary

Name   : Nelly   Age : 48
Owner : Buck, Maria   And   William R.
Year   : 1846/08/27   Page: 038

Name   : Nelly   Age : 35
Owner : Shanahan, Elizabeth And Timothy
Year   : 1848/06/01   Page: 049
Note: Nelly was purchased from Hezekiah M. Bassett on April 14.

Name   : Nero   Age : 45
Owner : McIntyre, Emily   And   Thomas G.
Year   : 1848/01/15   Page: 045

Name   : Nero Junior   Age : 6
Owner : McIntyre, Emily   And   Thomas G.
Year   : 1848/01/15   Page: 045

Name   : Nicey   Age : 27
Owner : Brown, Ann   And   Thomas W.

PORT GIBSON PROPERTY
LIST 1846-1858

Nicey(cont)
Year   : 1846/04/29   Page: 001
Husband : Shadrack
Children : Little Betsey and Sophia.
Note: Ann Brown was heir of Ralph Regan.

Name   : Obe   Age : ?
Owner : Mitchell, Harriet And John
Year   : 1857/09/22   Page: 061

Name   : Olevia   Age : 1
Owner   : Snodgrass, Margaret And John
Year   : 1846/08/24   Page: 036
Mother : Harriet Ann
Sibling : Clem and Chaney.

Name   : Oliva   Age : 17
Owner : Coleman, Catharine And John
Year   : 1857/04/18   Page: 061

Name   : Olmstead   Age : 17
Owner : Shaifer, Clarissa And Henry T.
Year   : 1852/06/24   Page: 062

Name   : Oscar   Age : 4
Owner : McIntyre, Emily And Thomas G.
Year   : 1848/01/15   Page: 045

Name   : Pallis   Age : 26
Owner : Clarke, Martha And Elijah L.
Year   : 1846/02/28   Page: 031

Name   : Pandora   Age : 36
Owner : Coleman, Catharine And John
Year   : 1857/04/18   Page: 061

Name   : Paris   Age : .18
Owner : Rundell, Judith And Josiah Rundell
Year   : 1846/08/05   Page: 023
Mother : Louisa

Name   : Park   Age : 12
Owner : Sillers, Caroline And William

PORT GIBSON PROPERTY
LIST 1846-1858

Park (cont)
Year   : 1846/07/22   Page: 018
Mother : Cely
Sibling : Wash, Mary, Betsy, Hester and Amos.

Name   : Parthena   Age : ?
Owner   : Patton, Malinda   And   Francis
Year   : 1846/06/26   Page: 006

Name   : Patience   Age : ?
Owner   : Strong, Malinda   And   George P.
Year   : 1846/05/30   Page: 004

Name   : Patsey   Age : 35
Owner   : Buck, Maria   And   William R.
Year   : 1846/08/27   Page: 038

Name   : Patsey   Age : 2
Owner   : Margaret, Snodgrass And John
Year   : 1846/08/24   Page: 036

Name   : Patsy   Age : 27
Owner   : Brown, Ann   And   Thomas W.
Year   : 1846/04/29   Page: 001
Note: Ann Brown was heir of Ralph Regan.

Name   : Patsy   Age : ?
Owner   : Mitchell, Harriet And John
Year   : 1857/09/22   Page: 061

Name   : Patsy   Age : 2
Owner   : Snodgrass, Margaret And John
Year   : 1846/08/24   Page: 036

Name   : Peggy   Age : ?
Owner   : Bland, Emeline   And   Maxwell W.
Year   : 1846/08/04   Page: 024

Name   : Peter   Age : 25
Owner   : Buck, Maria   And   William R.
Year   : 1846/08/27   Page: 038

Name   : Pheby   Age : 22

PORT GIBSON PROPERTY
LIST 1846-1858

Pheby(cont)
Owner : McAlphine, Sally And William H.
Year : 1854/01/01   Page: 077

Name : Plummer   Age : 13
Owner : McIntyre, Emily And Thomas G.
Year : 1848/01/15   Page: 045

Name : Polly   Age : 35
Owner : Marye, Mary P. And James T.
Year : 1846/08/18   Page: 032

Name : Polly   Age : 15
Owner : McIntyre, Emily And Thomas G.
Year : 1848/01/15   Page: 045

Name : Powell   Age : 15
Owner : Chambliss, Elizabeth And Cortez
Year : 1847/10/13   Page: 063

Name   : Priscilla   Age : 2
Owner : Spencer, Sarah A. And H. W.
Year   : 1846/02/28   Page: 008
Mother : Cynthia
Sibling: Ellen, Cora, Aruelia and Jeffrey.

Name : Puss   Age : 15
Owner : McIntyre, Emily And Thomas G.
Year : 1848/01/15   Page: 045

Name : Rachel   Age : ?
Owner : Bland, Emeline And Maxwell W.
Year : 1846/08/04   Page: 024

Name : Rachel   Age : 60
Owner : Brown, Ann And Thomas W.
Year : 1846/04/29   Page: 001
Note: Rachel was related to Moses, Mira And Nancy. Ann Brown was heir of Ralph Regan.

Name : Rachel   Age : 27
Owner : McIntyre, Emily And Thomas G.
Year : 1848/01/15   Page: 045

PORT GIBSON PROPERTY
LIST 1846-1858

Name   : Ralph   Age : 8
Owner   : Sillers, Caroline And William
Year   : 1846/07/22   Page: 018
Parents : Bill And Mary Ann
Siblingse: Martha, Van Buren and Joseph.

Name   : Ralph Sr.   Age : 37
Owner   : Sillers, Caroline And William
Year   : 1846/07/22   Page: 018

Name   : Ramsey   Age : 15
Owner   : Gordon, Candis And Johnson W.
Year   : 1846/08/03   Page: 022

Name   : Raney   Age : .7
Owner   : Bobo, Eliza M. And Absalom H.
Year   : 1846/08/12   Page: 029
Mother : Ellen
Sibling : Bill

Name   : Raney   Age : 16
Owner   : Hamer, Amazon And William H.
Year   : 1846/08/01   Page: 027
Child   : Eight months old Infant.

Name   : Ransom   Age : ?
Owner   : Mitchell, Harriet And John
Year   : 1857/09/22   Page: 061

Name   : Raymond   Age : 15
Owner   : Clarke, Martha And Elijah L.
Year   : 1846/02/28   Page: 031
Note: Raymond was the property of The William Ervin Estate.

Name   : Rhody   Age : ?
Owner   : Rossman, Hariet And Dr. Walter
Year   : 1846/07/21   Page: 017

Name   : Richard   Age : 18
Owner   : McIntyre, Emily And Thomas G.
Year   : 1848/01/15   Page: 045

PORT GIBSON PROPERTY LIST 1846-1858

Name : Rob   Age : 60
Owner : Coleman, Catharine And John
Year : 1857/04/18   Page: 061

Name : Roberson   Age : ?
Owner : Patton, Malinda And Francis
Year : 1846/06/26   Page: 006

Name : Robert   Age : 35
Owner : Brown, Ann And Thomas W.
Year : 1846/04/29   Page: 001
Note: Ann Brown was heir of Ralph Regan.

Name : Robin   Age : ?
Owner : Patton, Malinda And Francis
Year : 1846/06/26   Page: 006

Name : Rose   Age : 40
Owner : Brock, Vashti And Valentine W.
Year : 1848/05/23   Page: 048
Husband : Bill
Note: Vashti was heir of A. Brook from Louisiana.

Name : Rose   Age : 49
Owner : Clarke, Martha And Elijah L.
Year : 1846/02/28   Page: 031
Note: Rose was property of The William Ervin Estate.

Name : Rose   Age : 17
Owner : Forbes, Sarah Ann And Spooner
Year : 1846/08/14   Page: 026

Name : Rose   Age : 20
Owner : McGilvary, Mary And Alexander
Year : 1846/08/18   Page: 030
Children: Aaron, Santre and Albert.

Name : Roseann   Age : 31
Owner : Clarke, Martha And Elijah L.
Year : 1846/02/28   Page: 031
Note: Property of the William Ervin Estate.

PORT GIBSON PROPERTY
LIST 1846-1858

Name : Roy   Age : 14
Owner : Buck, Maria   And William R.
Year : 1846/08/27   Page: 038

Name : Sally   Age : 40
Owner : McDougall, Elizabeth And Nicholas
Year : 1846/08/13   Page: 025

Name : Sally   Age : 28
Owner : McIntyre, Emily And Thomas G.
Year : 1848/01/15   Page: 045

Name : Saluda   Age : ?
Owner : Patton, Malinda And Francis
Year : 1846/06/26   Page: 006

Name : Sam   Age : ?
Owner : Brock, Vashti And Valentine W.
Year : 1848/05/23   Page: 048
Mother : Eliza
Siblings: Mariah, Matilda, Courtney, Hariet,
          Chapurnur and Elizabeth.
Note: Vashti was heir of A. Brook from
Louisiana.

Name : Sam   Age : 2
Owner : Brown, Ann   And Thomas W.
Year : 1846/04/29   Page: 001
Note: Ann Brown was heir of Ralph Regan.

Name : Sam   Age : 12
Owner : Buck, Maria   And William R.
Year : 1846/08/27   Page: 038

Name : Sam   Age : ?
Owner : Chambliss, Mary And Calvin T.
Year : 1852/08/09   Page: 066

Name : Sam   Age : 30
Owner : McAlphine, Sally And William H.
Year : 1854/01/01   Page: 077

Name : Sam   Age : 30

PORT GIBSON PROPERTY LIST 1846-1858

Sam (cont)
Owner : McAlphine, Sally And William H.
Year : 1854/01/01   Page: 077
Note: Sam was called "Big" Sam.

Name : Sam   Age : 25
Owner : McAlphine, Sally And William H.
Year : 1854/01/01   Page: 077
Note: Sam was called "Little" Sam.

Name   : Sam   Age : 38
Owner   : Sims, Emeline F. And Isaac A.
Year   : 1847/03/25   Page: 042
Wife   : Sylva
Children: Little Fanny, Crack, Manda Child, 6 months.

Name : Sandy   Age : ?
Owner : Rossman, Hariet And Dr. Walter
Year : 1846/07/21   Page: 017

Name   : Santre   Age : 4
Owner : McGilvary, Mary And Alexander
Year   : 1846/08/18   Page: 030
Mother : Rose
Sibling: Aaron and Albert.

Name : Sarah   Age : 20
Owner : Clarke, Martha And Elijah L.
Year : 1846/02/28   Page: 031
Child : Susan
Note: Sarah was the property of The William Ervin Estate.

Name : Sarah   Age : 1
Owner : Coleman, Catharine And John
Year : 1857/04/18   Page: 061

Name : Sarah   Age : 24
Owner : Gage, Rosanna And James A.
Year : 1846/07/20   Page: 016

Name : Sarah   Age : 4

PORT GIBSON PROPERTY
LIST 1846-1858

Sarah(cont)
Owner : Magrunder, Sarah And Dr. Thomas B.
Year : 1852/08/14   Page: 067

Name   : Sarah   Age : 24
Owner   : McDougall, Susan And Daniel
Year   : 1853/02/02   Page: 070
Children: Elsey and Lucy.
Note: Elsey was Mulatto.

Name : Sarah   Age : ?
Owner : Mitchell, Harriet And John
Year : 1857/09/22   Page: 061

Name : Sarah   Age : 19
Owner : Moore, Permelia And Rich M.
Year : 1846/07/18   Page: 015

Name : Sarah   Age : 35
Owner : Sayer, Harriet B. And William D.
Year : 1847/03/03   Page: 041

Name   : Sarah   Age : ?
Owner   : Stamps, Jane   And Volney
Year   : 1846/08/03   Page: 021
Children: Billy and Kate.

Name : Sarah   Age : 9
Owner : Thomson, Elizabeth And Thomas W.
Year : 1846/07/02   Page: 013

Name : Sarinia   Age : 13
Owner : Coleman, Catharine And John
Year : 1857/04/18   Page: 061

Name   : Shadrack   Age : 40
Owner   : Brown, Ann   And Thomas W.
Year   : 1846/04/29   Page: 001
Wife   : Nicey
Children: Little Betsey and Sophia.
Note: Ann Brown was heir of Ralph Regan.

Name : Sharper   Age : 50

PORT GIBSON PROPERTY
LIST 1846-1858

Sharper(cont)
Owner : McIntyre, Emily And Thomas G.
Year : 1848/01/15   Page: 045

Name : Sidney   Age : 6
Owner : Hamer, Amazon   And William H.
Year : 1846/08/01   Page: 027

Name : Sidney   Age : 33
Owner : McIntyre, Emily And Thomas G.
Year : 1848/01/15   Page: 045

Name : Sillers   Age : ?
Owner : Bland, Emeline   And Maxwell W.
Year : 1846/08/04   Page: 024

Name : Silva   Age : 6
Owner : Buck, Maria   And William R.
Year : 1846/08/27   Page: 038

Name : Silva   Age : ?
Owner : Mitchell, Harriet And John
Year : 1857/09/22   Page: 061

Name : Silvia   Age : 11
Owner : Coleman, Catharine And John
Year : 1857/04/18   Page: 061

Name : Simon   Age : 45
Owner : Brock, Vashti   And Valentine W.
Year : 1848/05/23   Page: 048
Note: Vashti was heir of A. Brook from Louisiana.

Name : Simon   Age : 40
Owner : Magrunder, Sarah And Dr. Thomas B.
Year : 1852/08/14   Page: 067

Name   : Sophia   Age : 4
Owner : Brown, Ann   And Thomas W.
Year   : 1846/04/29   Page: 001
Father : Shadrack
Mother : Nicey

PORT GIBSON PROPERTY
LIST 1846-1858

Sophia (cont)
Sibling : Little Betsy.
Note: **Ann** Brown was heir of Ralph Regan.

Name   : Sophy   Age : 35
Owner : Snodgrass, Margaret And John
Year   : 1846/08/24   Page: 036

Name   : Spencer   Age : 13
Owner : Brown, Ann   And Thomas W.
Year   : 1846/04/29   Page: 001
Note: Ann Brown was heir of Ralph Regan.
Spencer was called "Little" Spencer.

Name   : Spencer   Age : 25
Owner : Brown, Ann   And Thomas W.
Year   : 1846/04/29   Page: 001
Note: Ann **Brown Wws** heir of Ralph Regan.
Spencer was called "Big" Spencer.

Name   : Spencer   Age : 34
Owner : Clarke, Martha And Elijah L.
Year   : 1846/02/28   Page: 031
Note: Spencer was the property of The William Ervin Estate.

Name   : Stephen   Age : 50
Owner : Buck, Maria   And William R.
Year   : 1846/08/27   Page: 038

Name   : Stephen   Age : 20
Owner : McIntyre, Emily And Thomas G.
Year   : 1848/01/15   Page: 045

Name   : Susan   Age : 8
Owner : Brown, Ann   And Thomas W.
Year   : 1846/04/29   Page: 001
Note: Ann Brown was heir of Ralph Regan.

Name   : Susan   Age : 29
Owner : Brown, Ann   And Thomas W.
Year   : 1854/08/09   Page: 076

PORT GIBSON PROPERTY
LIST 1846-1858

Name   : Susan   Age : 2
Owner : Clarke, Martha   And Elijah L.
Year   : 1846/02/28   Page: 031
Mother : Sarah.
Note: Susan was the property of The William Ervin Estate.

Name   : Susan   Age : 30
Owner : Clarke, Martha   And Elijah L.
Year   : 1846/02/28   Page: 031

Name   : Susan   Age : 13
Owner : Coleman, Catharine And John
Year   : 1857/04/18   Page: 061

Name   : Susan   Age : ?
Owner : Patton, Malinda And Francis
Year   : 1846/06/26   Page: 006

Name   : Susan   Age : 14
Owner : Shaifer, Clarissa And Henry T.
Year   : 1852/06/24   Page: 062

Name   : Susan   Age : ?
Owner : Tebo, Ann C.   And William B.
Year   : 1846/06/27   Page: 013

Name   : Sutt   Age : 13
Owner : McDougall, Ann E. And Duncan
Year   : 1846/07/02   Page: 006
Note: Sutt was a Mulatto girl.

Name   : Suzette   Age : 17
Owner   : Shaifer, Elizabeth And Abram K.
Year   : 1846/06/10   Page: 003
Parents : William and Mary
Siblings: Cyrus, Amerricus and Mary Ann.

Name   : Sylva   Age : 9
Owner : Sayer, Harriet B. And William D.
Year   : 1847/03/03   Page: 041

Name   : Sylva   Age : 30

PORT GIBSON PROPERTY
LIST 1846-1858

Sylva(cont)
Owner   : Sims, Emeline F. And Isaac A.
Year   : 1847/03/25   Page: 042
Husband : Sam
Children : Little Fanny, Crack, Manda child 6 months old.

Name : Tabitha   Age : ?
Owner : Mitchell, Harriet And John
Year : 1857/09/22   Page: 061

Name : Taswell   Age : 1
Owner : Wilson, Elizabeth And Charles W.
Year : 1846/07/31   Page: 019

Name : Teaner   Age : ?
Owner : Patton, Malinda And Francis
Year : 1846/06/26   Page: 006

Name : Tempe   Age : 20
Owner : McAlphine, Sally And William H.
Year : 1854/01/01   Page: 077

Name : Tena   Age : 31
Owner : Hamer, Amazon   And William H.
Year : 1846/08/01   Page: 027

Name : Tenner   Age : 55
Owner : McGilvary, Mary And Alexander
Year : 1846/08/18   Page: 030

Name : Tennessee   Age : 10
Owner : McIntyre, Emily And Thomas G.
Year : 1848/01/15   Page: 045

Name : Tilda   Age : 16
Owner : Brown, Ann   And Thomas W.
Year : 1846/04/29   Page: 001
Note: Ann Brown was heir of Ralph Regan.

Name : Tillis   Age : 45
Owner : McIntyre, Emily And Thomas G.
Year : 1848/01/15   Page: 045

PORT GIBSON PROPERTY LIST 1846-1858

```
Name   : Tom                        Age : 12
Owner  : Brown, Ann        And  Thomas W.
Year   : 1846/04/29                 Page: 001
Note: Ann Brown was heir of Ralph Regan.

Name   : Tom                        Age : 60
Owner  : Chambliss, Elizabeth And  Cortez
Year   : 1847/10/13                 Page: 063

Name   : Tom                        Age : ?
Owner  : Chambliss, Mary   And  Calvin T.
Year   : 1852/08/09                 Page: 066

Name   : Tom                        Age : 12
Owner  : McIntyre, Emily   And  Thomas G.
Year   : 1848/01/15                 Page: 045

Name   : Tom                        Age : 7
Owner  : Patterson, Louise And  James H.
Year   : 1854/05/02                 Page: 074
Note:Tom was Conveyed by Sam Peosis, Bookz
Pages 172 & 173.

Name   : Tom                        Age : 2
Owner  : Shaifer, Clarissa And  Henry T.
Year   : 1852/06/24                 Page: 062

Name   : Tom                        Age : ?
Owner  : Strong, Malinda   And  George P.
Year   : 1846/05/30                 Page: 004

Name   : Tom                        Age : 3
Owner  : Thomson, Caroline And  Benjamin W.
Year   : 1852/06/14                 Page: 065
Mother : Emily

Name   : Tony                       Age : .5
Owner  : Brown, Ann        And  Thomas W.
Year   : 1846/04/29                 Page: 001
Note: Tony was related to Charity, Willis and
Henry. Ann Brown was heir of Ralph Regan.

Name   : Van Buren                  Age : 11
```

PORT GIBSON PROPERTY
LIST 1846-1858

Van Buren(cont)
Owner   : Sillers, Caroline And William
Year   : 1846/07/22   Page: 018
Parents : Bill and Mary Ann
Sibling : Martha, Ralph Jr. and Joseph.

Name   : Victoria   Age : ?
Owner   : Stamps, Jane   And Volney
Year   : 1846/08/03   Page: 021
Mother : Eliza
Sibling : Junius, Crockett, Humphreys Albert,
          and Ina.

Name   : Ving   Age : ?
Owner   : Bland, Emeline   And Maxwell W.
Year   : 1846/08/04   Page: 024

Name   : Violet   Age : 45
Owner   : Shanahan, Elizabeth And Timothy
Year   : 1848/06/01   Page:
Note: Purchased from Hezekiah M. Bussett or
Bassett On April 14 ?

Name   : Wash   Age : 16
Owner   : Sillers, Caroline And William
Year   : 1846/07/22   Page: 018
Mother : Cely
Sibling : Ebb, Park, Mary, Betsy, Hester.

Name   : Washington   Age : ?
Owner   : Mitchell, Harriet And John
Year   : 1857/09/22   Page: 061

Name   : Washington   Age : ?
Owner   : Patton, Malinda And Francis
Year   : 1846/06/26   Page: 006

Name   : Wesley   Age : ?
Owner   : Patton, Malinda And Francis
Year   : 1846/06/26   Page: 006

Name   : Wilda   Age : 13
Owner   : Buck, Maria   And William R.

PORT GIBSON PROPERTY
LIST 1846-1858

Wilda(cont)
Year   : 1846/08/27   Page: 038

Name   : Will   Age : ?
Owner   : Patton, Malinda And Francis
Year   : 1846/06/26   Page: 006

Name   : Will   Age : 76
Owner   : Spencer, Sarah A. And H. W.
Year   : 1846/02/28   Page: 008

Name   : William   Age : ?
Owner   : Bland, Emeline   And Maxwell W.
Year   : 1846/08/04   Page: 024

Name   : William   Age : .8
Owner   : Clarke, Martha   And Elijah L.
Year   : 1846/02/28   Page: 031
Note: William was the property of The William Ervin Estate.

Name   : William   Age : 3
Owner   : Coleman, Catharine And John
Year   : 1857/04/18   Page: 061

Name   : William   Age : 55
Owner   : Shaifer, Elizabeth And Abram K.
Year   : 1846/06/10   Page: 003
Wife   : Mary
Children: Cyrus, Suzette, Amerricus, and
          Mary Ann.

Name   : Willis   Age : ?
Owner   : Bland, Emeline   And Maxwell W.
Year   : 1846/08/04   Page: 024

Name   : Willis   Age : 18
Owner   : Brown, Ann   And Thomas W.
Year   : 1846/04/29   Page: 001
Note: Willis was related to Charity, Henry And Jony. Ann Brown was heir of Ralph Regan.

Name   : Willis   Age : ?

PORT GIBSON PROPERTY LIST 1846-1858

Willis(cont)
Owner : Chambliss, Mary And Calvin T.
Year : 1852/08/09   Page: 066

Name : Willis   Age : 43
Owner : Clarke, Martha   And Elijah L.
Year : 1846/08/20   Page: 031

Name : Willoby   Age : ?
Owner : Rossman, Hariet   And Dr. Walter
Year : 1846/07/21   Page: 017

Name : Wilson   Age : 36
Owner : McIntyre, Emily   And Thomas G.
Year : 1848/01/15   Page: 045

Name : Winny   Age : 33
Owner : McIntyre, Emily   And Thomas G.
Year : 1848/01/15   Page: 045

Name : Wlliam   Age : 4
Owner : McIntyre, Emily   And Thomas G.
Year : 1848/01/15   Page: 045

Name : York   Age : 28
Owner : McIntyre, Emily   And Thomas G.
Year : 1848/01/15   Page: 045

Name : Zilean   Age : 4
Owner : Hamer, Amazon   And William H.
Year : 1846/08/01   Page: 027

CERTIFICATE FOR SLAVE SALE

```
Name    : Abell
Traders : Miller, John & Mattingly, William
Date    : 1859/10/11
City    : Marion               State : KY

Name    : Adaline
Traders : Hunter, John & Mattingly, William
Date    : 1860/01/05
City    : St. Louis            State : MO

Name    : Adam
Traders : Hunter, John & Mattingly, William
Date    : 1859/09/21
City    : St. Louis            State : MO

Name    : Adeline
Traders : Hunter, John & Mattingly, William
Date    : 1860/01/05
City    : St. Louis            State : MO

Name    : Agnes?
Traders : Miller, John
Date    : 1860/08/29           Age   : 4
City    : Nelson County        State : KY
Mother  : Amanda
Sibling : George

Name    : Agnez
Traders : Mobley, Orran & Deas, Ephraim
Date    : 1859/12/23
City    : Shelby County        State : KY
Note: Agnez belonged to James Myers.

Name    : Alex
Traders : Miller, John & Mattingly, William
Date    : 1859/10/11
City    : Marion               State : KY

Name    : Alford
Traders : Huges, R. D.
Date    : 1860/09/14
City    : Memphis              State : TN
```

CERTIFICATE FOR SLAVE SALE

Name   : Alfred
Traders : Alexander, C. L.
Date   : 1858/12/04
City   : St. Louis   State : MO

Name   : Alfred
Traders : Miller, John & Mattingly, William
Date   : 1859/10/11
City   : Marion   State : KY

Name   : Alfred Wiseheart
Traders : Miller, John
Date   : 1858/12/28
City   : Nelson   State : KY

Name   : Alick
Traders : Hunter, John & Mattingly, William
Date   : 1859/01/24
City   : St. Louis   State : MO

Name   : Alliace
Traders : Alexander, C. L.
Date   : 1859/01/24
City   : St. Louis   State : MO

Name   : Amanda
Traders : Miller, John
Date   : 1860/08/29   Age   : 28
City   : Nelson County   State : KY
Children : Agnes? and George.

Name   : Amanda Jenkins
Traders : Miller, John
Date   : 1859/01/27   Age   : 27
City   : Nelson County   State : KY

Name   : America
Traders : Huges, R. D.
Date   : 1860/09/14
City   : Memphis   State : TN

Name   : America
Traders : Hunter, John

CERTIFICATE FOR SLAVE SALE

America (cont)
Date   : 1859/03/13
City   : St. Louis   State : MO

Name   : Amios
Traders : Hunter, John & Mattingly, William
Date   : 1859/10/04
City   : St. Louis   State : MO

Name   : Amy
Traders : Hunter, John & Mattingly, William
Date   : 1859/01/24
City   : St. Louis   State : MO

Name   : Andrew
Traders : Alexander, C. L.
Date   : 1859/02/07
City   : St. Louis   State : MO

Name   : Andrew
Traders : Hunter, John & Mattingly, William
Date   : 1859/01/24
City   : St. Louis   State : MO

Name   : Anemeda
Traders : Hunter, John & Mattingly, William
Date   : 1859/09/21
City   : St. Louis   State : MO

Name   : Angeline
Traders : Alexander, C. L.
Date   : 1859/01/08
City   : St. Louis   State : MO

Name   : Ann
Traders : Alexander, C. L.
Date   : 1859/01/08
City   : St. Louis   State : MO

Name   : Ann
Traders : Hunter, John & Mattingly, William
Date   : 1859/09/21
City   : St. Louis   State : MO

CERTIFICATE FOR SLAVE SALE

Name   : Ann
Traders : Hunter, John & Mattingly, William
Date   : 1859/10/04
City   : St. Louis   State : MO
Note: There were three(3) women named Ann listed. One was noted as having a child and another listed as having an infant. Their ages were not given.

Name   : Ann
Traders : Hunter, John & Mattingly, William
Date   : 1860/01/05
City   : St. Louis   State : MO

Name   : Ann
Traders : Hunter, John & Mattingly, William
Date   : 1859/01/24
City   : St. Louis   State : MO

Name   : Ann
Traders : Miller, John & Mattingly, William
Date   : 1859/10/11
City   : Marion   State : KY

Name   : Ann
Traders : Miller, John
Date   : 1860/08/29   Age   : 14
City   : Nelson County   State : KY

Name   : Ann Rilda
Traders : Hunter, John & Mattingly, William
Date   : 1859/09/21
City   : St. Louis   State : MO

Name   : Antony
Traders : Hunter, John & Mattingly, William
Date   : 1859/01/24
City   : St. Louis   State : MO

Name   : Arrilla
Traders : Hunter, John & Mattingly, William
Date   : 1860/01/05
City   : St. Louis   State : MO

CERTIFICATE FOR SLAVE SALE

Name   : Arthur
Traders : Hunter, John & Mattingly, William
Date   : 1859/09/21
City   : St. Louis   State   : MO

Name   : Barbara
Traders : Hunter, John & Mattingly, William
Date   : 1859/01/24
City   : St. Louis   State   : MO

Name   : Barry
Traders : Hunter, John & Mattingly, William
Date   : 1859/10/04
City   : St. Louis   State   : MO

Name   : Battees?
Traders : Alexander, C. L.
Date   : 1859/02/07
City   : St. Louis   State   : MO

Name   : Bein
Traders : Hunter, John & Mattingly, William
Date   : 1859/10/04
City   : St. Louis   State   : MO

Name   : Ben
Traders : Hunter, John & Mattingly, William
Date   : 1859/10/04
City   : St. Louis   State   : MO

Name   : Ben Hayden
Traders : Miller, John
Date   : 1859/01/31   Age   : 23
City   : Nelson   State   : KY

Name   : Benn
Traders : Alexander, C. L.
Date   : 1859/02/07
City   : St. Louis   State   : MO

Name   : Benton
Traders : Hunter, John & Mattingly, William
Date   : 1860/01/05

CERTIFICATE FOR SLAVE SALE

Benton (cont)
City   : St. Louis   State   : MO

Name   : Bess
Traders : McDaniel, Robertson J.
Date   : 1859/11/26
City   : St. Louis   State   : MO

Name   : Betty
Traders : Alexander, C. L.
Date   : 1859/03/12
City   : Memphis   State   : TN

Name   : Bill
Traders : Hunter, John & Mattingly, William
Date   : 1859/01/24
City   : St. Louis   State   : MO

Name   : Bill
Traders : Miller, John
Date   : 1859/01/27   Age   : 18
City   : Nelson   State   : KY

Name   : Bill Humphry
Traders : Miller, John
Date   : 1858/12/28
City   : Nelson   State   : KY

Name   : Bob
Traders : Hunter, John & Mattingly, William
Date   : 1859/10/04
City   : St. Louis   State   : MO

Name   : Bob
Traders : Hunter, John & Mattingly, William
Date   : 1859/12/06
City   : St. Louis   State   : MO

Name   : Bob
Traders : Hunter, John & Mattingly, William
Date   : 1859/01/24
City   : St. Louis   State   : MO

CERTIFICATE FOR SLAVE SALE

Name   : Caezar
Traders : Alexander, C. L.
Date   : 1859/03/12
City   : Memphis   State : TN

Name   : Caroline
Traders : Alexander, C. L.
Date   : 1859/03/12
City   : Memphis   State : TN
Note: Caroline had a child.

Name   : Caroline
Traders : Hunter, John & Mattingly, William
Date   : 1860/01/05
City   : St. Louis   State : MO

Name   : Caroline
Traders : Middleton, Anthony & Stratton, C. M.
          Gloyd, B.F.
Date   : 1860/02/06
City   : Shelby County   State : KY
Note: Caroline belonged to Adam Maron Middleton.

Name   : Catharine
Traders : Hunter, John & Mattingly, William
Date   : 1860/01/05
City   : St. Louis   State : MO

Name   : Catharine Williams
Traders : Miller, John
Date   : 1858/12/8
City   : Nelson   State : KY

Name   : Charity
Traders : Hunter, John & Mattingly, William
Date   : 1859/01/24
City   : St. Louis   State : MO

Name   : Charles
Traders : Hunter, John & Mattingly, William
Date   : 1860/01/05
City   : St. Louis   State : MO

CERTIFICATE FOR SLAVE SALE

Name   : Charles
Traders : Miller, John
Date   : 1860/08/29   Age   : 25
City   : Nelson County   State : KY

Name   : Charles Phillips
Traders : Miller, John
Date   : 1858/12/28
City   : Nelson   State : KY

Name   : Charley
Traders : Hunter, John & Mattingly, William
Date   : 1859/10/04
City   : St. Louis   State : MO

Name   : Charlie Cuns?
Traders : Alexander, C. L.
Date   : 1858/12/04
City   : St. Louis   State : MO

Name   : Charlotte Grundy?
Traders : Miller, John
Date   : 1858/12/28
City   : Nelson   State : KY

Name   : Clara
Traders : Alexander, C. L.
Date   : 1858/04/23
City   : St. Louis   State : MO

Name   : Clarissa
Traders : Miller, John
Date   : 1860/08/29   Age   : 13
City   : Nelson County   State : KY

Name   : Corneal
Traders : Alexander, C. L.
Date   : 1859/01/24
City   : St. Louis   State : MO

Name   : Crockett
Traders : Alexander, C. L.
Date   : 1858/12/04

CERTIFICATE FOR SLAVE SALE

Crockett(cont)
City   : St. Louis   State : MO

Name   : Daniel
Traders : Alexander, C. L.
Date   : 1858/04/23
City   : St. Louis   State : MO

Name   : Daniel
Traders : Hunter, John, Mattingly, William
Date   : 1859/01/24
City   : St. Louis   State : MO

Name   : Dankeys
Traders : Alexander, C. L.
Date   : 1858/04/23
City   : St. Louis   State : MO

Name   : Dave Graves
Traders : Miller, John
Date   : 1858/12/28
City   : Nelson   State : KY

Name   : David
Traders : Alexander, C. L.
Date   : 1859/02/07
City   : St. Louis   State : MO

Name   : David
Traders : Hunter, John & Mattingly, William
Date   : 1859/09/21
City   : St. Louis   State : MO

Name   : David
Traders : Hunter, John & Mattingly, William
Date   : 1859/10/04
City   : St. Louis   State : MO

Name   : David Jarrosp?
Traders : Hunter, John & Mattingly, William
Date   : 1859/09/21
City   : St. Louis   State : MO

CERTIFICATE FOR SLAVE SALE

Name   : Diana
Traders : Hunter, John & Mattingly, William
Date   : 1859/09/21
City   : St. Louis   State : MO
Note: Diana had a child.

Name   : Dick
Traders : Alexander, C. L.
Date   : 1859/03/12
City   : Memphis   State : TN

Name   : Dick
Traders : Hunter, John
Date   : 1859/01/08
City   : St. Louis   State : MO

Name   : Dick
Traders : Hunter, John & Mattingly, William
Date   : 1859/01/24
City   : St. Louis   State : MO

Name   : Dill
Traders : Alexander, C. L.
Date   : 1859/03/12
City   : Memphis   State : TN

Name   : Dolly
Traders : Smyth, A.
Date   : 1849/02/24   Age   : 42
City   : Port Gibson   State : MS
Note: Dolly was sold to Mary D. Moody.

Name   : Dorcus
Traders : Alexander, C. L.
Date   : 1859/03/19
City   : Memphis   State : TN

Name   : Drake
Traders : Alexander, C. L.
Date   : 1858/12/04
City   : St. Louis   State : MO

Name   : Drucilla

CERTIFICATE FOR SLAVE SALE

Traders : Alexander, C. L.
Date   : 1859/03/12
City   : Memphis   State : TN

Name   : Ed
Traders : Hunter, John & Mattingly, William
Date   : 1859/12/06
City   : St. Louis   State : MO

Name   : Edmond
Traders : Hunter, John & Mattingly, William
Date   : 1859/01/24
City   : St. Louis   State : MO

Name   : Edy
Traders : Hunter, John & Mattingly, William
Date   : 1859/09/21
City   : St. Louis   State : MO

Name   : Elick
Traders : Hunter, John & Mattingly, William
Date   : 1859/09/21
City   : St. Louis   State : MO

Name   : Elinysa
Traders : Hunter, John & Mattingly, William
Date   : 1859/09/21
City   : St. Louis   State : MO

Name   : Eliza
Traders : Alexander, C. L.
Date   : 1859/03/19
City   : Memphis   State : TN

Name   : Eliza
Traders : Hunter, John & Mattingly, William
Date   : 1859/09/21
City   : St. Louis   State : MO

Name   : Eliza
Traders : Hunter, John
Date   : 1859/01/08

CERTIFICATE FOR SLAVE SALE

Eliza(cont)
City   : St. Louis   State   : MO

Name   : Eliza
Traders : Hunter, John & Mattingly, William
Date   : 1859/01/24
City   : St. Louis   State   : MO

Name   : Eliza
Traders : Hunter, William
Date   : 1859/03/13
City   : St. Louis   State   : MO

Name   : Eliza Baker
Traders : Miller, John
Date   : 1858/12/28
City   : Nelson   State   : KY

Name   : Eliza Jane
Traders : Alexander, C. L.
Date   : 1858/12/04
City   : St. Louis   State   : MO

Name   : Elizabeth
Traders : Hunter, John & Mattingly, William
Date   : 1859/09/21
City   : St. Louis   State   : MO

Name   : Elizabeth
Traders : Hunter, John & Mattingly, William
Date   : 1859/01/24
City   : St. Louis   State   : MO

Name   : Elizabeth Ann
Traders : Alexander, C. L.
Date   : 1858/12/04
City   : St. Louis   State   : MO

Name   : Ellen Coleman
Traders : Miller, John
Date   : 1858/12/28
City   : Nelson   State   : KY

CERTIFICATE FOR SLAVE SALE

Name   : Emily
Traders : Huges, R. D.
Date   : 1860/09/14
City   : Memphis   State : TN

Name   : Emily
Traders : Hunter, John & Mattingly, William
Date   : 1859/09/21
City   : St. Louis   State : MO

Name   : Emily
Traders : Miller, John & Mattingly, William
Date   : 1859/10/11
City   : Marion   State : KY

Name   : Emily
Traders : Mobley, Orran
          Deas, Ephraim
Date   : 1859/12/23
City   : Shelby County   State : KY
Note: Emily belonged to James Myers.

Name   : Emmeline
Traders : Hunter, John & Mattingly, William
Date   : 1859/12/06
City   : St. Louis   State : MO

Name   : Fanney
Traders : Hunter, John & Mattingly, William
Date   : 1859/01/24
City   : St. Louis   State : MO

Name   : Fanny
Traders : McDaniel, Robertson J.
Date   : 1859/11/26
City   : St. Louis   State : MO

Name   : Fanny
Traders : Miller, John
Date   : 1860/08/29   Age   : 22
City   : Nelson County   State : KY
Note: Fanny had an eight months old infant.

CERTIFICATE FOR SLAVE SALE

Name   : Fanny Moss?
Traders : Miller, John
Date   : 1858/12/28
City   : Nelson   State   : KY

Name   : Fox
Traders : Alexander, C. L.
Date   : 1859/03/19
City   : Memphis   State   : TN

Name   : Frances
Traders : Alexander, C. L.
Date   : 1858/04/23   Age   : 21
City   : St. Louis   State   : MO
Note: Frances had a child.

Name   : Frances
Traders : McDaniel, Robertson J.
Date   : 1859/11/26
City   : St. Louis   State   : MO

Name   : Frances
Traders : Miller, John
Date   : 1859/01/14   Age   : 17
City   : Nelson County   State   : KY

Name   : Francis
Traders : Miller, John & Mattingly, William
Date   : 1859/10/11
City   : Marion   State   : KY

Name   : Frank
Traders : Hughes, R. D.
Date   : 1860/09/14
City   : Memphis   State   : TN

Name   : Frank
Traders : Hunter, John & Mattingly, William
Date   : 1859/09/21
City   : St. Louis   State   : MO

Name   : Frank
Traders : Hunter, John & Mattingly, William

CERTIFICATE FOR SLAVE SALE

Frank(cont)
Date : 1859/12/06
City : St. Louis   State : MO

Name   : Frank
Traders : Miller, John & Mattingly, William
Date   : 1859/10/11
City   : Marion   State : KY

Name   : Georga
Traders : Hunter, John & Mattingly, William
Date   : 1859/09/21
City   : St. Louis   State : MO

Name   : George
Traders : Alexander, C. L.
Date   : 1858/04/20
City   : Marion County   State : MO
Note: George was purchased from William Durinitt.?

Name   : George
Traders : Alexander, C. L.
Date   : 1859/01/24
City   : St. Louis   State : MO

Name   : George
Traders : Hughes, R. D.
Date   : 1860/09/14
City   : Memphis   State : TN

Name   : George
Traders : Hunter, John & Mattingly, William
Date   : 1859/10/04
City   : St. Louis   State : MO

Name   : George
Traders : Hunter, John & Mattingly, William
Date   : 1859/12/06
City   : St. Louis   State : MO

Name   : George
Traders : Hunter, John & Mattingly, William

CERTIFICATE FOR SLAVE SALE

George(cont)
Date   : 1859/01/24
City   : St. Louis   State   : MO

Name   : George
Traders : Miller, John & Mattingly, William
Date   : 1859/10/11
City   : Marion   State   : KY

Name   : George
Traders : Miller, John
Date   : 1860/08/29   Age   : .18
City   : Nelson County   State   : KY
Mother : Amanda
Sibling : Agnes

Name   : Gip?
Traders : Hunter, John
Date   : 1859/01/08
City   : St. Louis   State   : MO

Name   : Gizo ?
Traders : Hunter, John & Mattingly, William
Date   : 1859/10/04
City   : St. Louis   State   : MO

Name   : Grace
Traders : Hunter, John & Mattingly, William
Date   : 1859/01/24
City   : St. Louis   State   : MO

Name   : Grinus?
Traders : Alexander, C. L.
Date   : 1858/04/23
City   : St. Louis   State   : MO

Name   : Hanna
Traders : Hunter, John & Mattingly, William
Date   : 1859/09/21
City   : St. Louis   State   : MO

Name   : Hannah
Traders : Hunter, John & Mattingly, William

CERTIFICATE FOR SLAVE SALE

```
Date    : 1859/09/21
City    : St. Louis          State   : MO
Note: Hannah had a child.

Name    : Hannah Hayden
Traders : Miller, John
Date    : 1859/01/31         Age     : 40
City    : Nelson             State   : KY

Name    : Hariet
Traders : Hunter, John  & Mattingly, William
Date    : 1860/01/05
City    : St. Louis          State   : MO

Name    : Harriet
Traders : Hunter, John  & Mattingly, William
Date    : 1859/09/21
City    : St. Louis          State   : MO

Name    : Harriet
Traders : Hunter, John  & Mattingly, William
Date    : 1859/01/24
City    : St. Louis          State   : MO

Name    : Harriet
Traders : Jerman
Date    : 1858/01/08
City    : St. Louis          State   : MO
Husband : Sim
Note: Harriet and Sim had a child.

Name    : Harriett
Traders : Alexander, C. L.
Date    : 1859/03/19
City    : Memphis            State   : TN

Name    : Harriett
Traders : Hughes, R. D.
Date    : 1860/09/14
City    : Memphis            State   : TN

Name    : Harrison
Traders : Alexander, C. L.
```

CERTIFICATE FOR SLAVE SALE

Harrison(cont)
Date   : 1859/03/12
City   : Memphis   State   : TN

Name   : Harry
Traders : Hunter, John & Mattingly, William
Date   : 1859/01/24
City   : St. Louis   State   : MO

Name   : Harry Graves
Traders : Miller, John
Date   : 1858/12/28
City   : Nelson   State   : KY

Name   : Hary
Traders : Alexander, C. L.
Date   : 1858/04/23
City   : St. Louis   State   : MO

Name   : Henry
Traders : Alexander, C. L.
Date   : 1858/04/23   Age   : 20
City   : St. Louis   State   : MO

Name   : Henry
Traders : Huges, R. D.
Date   : 1860/09/14
City   : Memphis   State   : TN

Name   : Henry
Traders : Hunter, John & Mattingly, William
Date   : 1859/09/21
City   : St. Louis   State   : MO

Name   : Henry
Traders : Hunter, John & Mattingly, William
Date   : 1859/10/04
City   : St. Louis   State   : MO

Name   : Henry
Traders : Hunter, John & Mattingly, William
Date   : 1859/10/04
City   : St. Louis   State   : MO

CERTIFICATE FOR SLAVE SALE

Name   : Henry
Traders : Hunter, John & Mattingly, William
Date   : 1859/10/04
City   : St. Louis   State   : MO

Name   : Henry
Traders : Hunter, John & Mattingly, William
Date   : 1860/01/05
City   : St. Louis   State   : MO

Name   : Henry
Traders : Hunter, John
Date   : 1859/01/08
City   : St. Louis   State   : MO

Name   : Henry
Traders : Hunter, John & Mattingly, William
Date   : 1859/01/24
City   : St. Louis   State   : MO

Name   : Henry
Traders : Hunter, John & Mattingly, William
Date   : 1859/01/24
City   : St. Louis   State   : MO

Name   : Henry
Traders : McDaniel, Robertson J.
Date   : 1859/11/26
City   : St. Louis   State   : MO

Name   : Henry
Traders : Mobley, Orran & Deas, Ephraim
Date   : 1859/12/23
City   : Shelby County   State   : KY
Note: Henry belonged to James Myers.

Name   : Henry Garner
Traders : Alexander, C. L.
Date   : 1858/12/04
City   : St. Louis   State   : MO

Name   : Hiram
Traders : Hughes, R. D

CERTIFICATE FOR SLAVE SALE

Hiram(cont)
Date   : 1860/09/14
City   : Memphis   State   : TN

Name   : Ike
Traders : Hughes, R. D.
Date   : 1860/09/14
City   : Memphis   State   : TN

Name   : Isaac Thompson
Traders : Alexander, C. L.
Date   : 1858/12/04
City   : St. Louis   State   : MO

Name   : Isiah
Traders : McDaniel, Robertson J.
Date   : 1859/11/26
City   : St. Louis   State   : MO

Name   : Jack
Traders : Alexander, C. L.
Date   : 1858/04/28   Age   : 23
City   : St. Louis   State   : MO

Name   : Jack
Traders : Hunter, John & Mattingly, William
Date   : 1859/09/21
City   : St. Louis   State   : MO

Name   : Jack
Traders : Hunter, John & Mattingly, William
Date   : 1859/10/04
City   : St. Louis   State   : MO

Name   : Jackson
Traders : Hunter, John & Mattingly, William
Date   : 1859/01/24
City   : St. Louis   State   : MO

Name   : Jacob
Traders : Miller, John & Mattingly, William
Date   : 1859/10/11
City   : Marion   State   : KY

CERTIFICATE FOR SLAVE SALE

Name   : Jane
Traders : Alexander, C. L.
Date   : 1859/03/12
City   : Memphis   State : TN

Name   : Jane
Traders : Hughes, R. D
Date   : 1860/09/14
City   : Memphis   State : TN

Name   : Jane
Traders : Hunter, John & Mattingly, William
Date   : 1859/09/21
City   : St. Louis   State : MO

Name   : Jane
Traders : Hunter, John & Mattingly, William
Date   : 1859/12/06
City   : St. Louis   State : MO

Name   : Jane
Traders : McDaniel, Robertson J.
Date   : 1859/11/26
City   : St. Louis   State : MO

Name   : Jane
Traders : Miller, John & Mattingly, William
Date   : 1859/10/11
City   : Marion   State : KY

Name   : Jane
Traders : Miller, John
Date   : 1860/08/29   Age   : 13
City   : Nelson County   State : KY

Name   : Jane
Traders : Sarman, B. F.
Date   : 1859/08/24
City   : St. Louis   State : MO

Name   : Jane Bowin?
Traders : Alexander, C. L.
Date   : 1858/12/04

CERTIFICATE FOR SLAVE SALE

Jane Bowin (cont)
City   : St. Louis   State   : MO

Name   : Jiles
Traders : Hunter, John & Mattingly, William
Date   : 1860/01/05
City   : St. Louis   State   : MO

Name   : Jim
Traders : Alexander, C. L.
Date   : 1859/02/07
City   : St. Louis   State   : MO

Name   : Jim
Traders : Hunter, John & Mattingly, William
Date   : 1859/09/21
City   : St. Louis   State   : MO

Name   : Jim
Traders : Miller, John & Mattingly, William
Date   : 1859/10/11
City   : Marion   State   : KY

Name   : Jim
Traders : Miller, John
Date   : 1860/08/29   Age   : 20
City   : Nelson County   State   : KY

Name   : Jim Phillips
Traders : Miller, John
Date   : 1858/12/28
City   : Nelson   State   : KY

Name   : Jinny
Traders : Miller, John
Date   : 1860/08/29   Age   : 6
City   : Nelson County   State   : KY
Mother : Margaret

Name   : Jo
Traders : Hunter, John & Mattingly, William
Date   : 1859/01/24
City   : St. Louis   State   : MO

CERTIFICATE FOR SLAVE SALE

Name	: Jo		
Traders	: Miller, John		
Date	: 1860/08/29	Age	: 21
City	: Nelson County	State	: KY

Name   : Joe
Traders : Alexander, C. L.
Date   : 1859/03/12
City   : Memphis   State : TN

Name   : Joe
Traders : Hunter, John & Mattingly, William
Date   : 1859/09/21
City   : St. Louis   State : MO

Name   : John
Traders : Alexander, C. L.
Date   : 1859/03/12
City   : Memphis   State : TN

Name   : John
Traders : Hughes, R. D.
Date   : 1860/09/14
City   : Memphis   State : TN

Name   : John
Traders : Hunter, John & Mattingly, William
Date   : 1859/09/21
City   : St. Louis   State : MO

Name   : John
Traders : McDaniel, Robertson J.
Date   : 1859/11/26
City   : St. Louis   State : MO

Name	: John		
Traders	: Miller, John		
Date	: 1860/08/29	Age	: 27
City	: Nelson County	State	: KY

Name	: John		
Traders	: Miller, John		
Date	: 1860/08/29	Age	: 30

CERTIFICATE FOR SLAVE SALE

John (cont)
City   : Nelson County   State   : KY

Name   : John Bean
Traders : Miller, John
Date   : 1859/01/27   Age   : 20
City   : Nelson County   State   : KY

Name   : John Johnson
Traders : Miller, John
Date   : 1858/12/28
City   : Nelson   State   : KY

Name   : Jolowes?
Traders : Alexander, C. L.
Date   : 1859/02/07
City   : St. Louis   State   : MO

Name   : Joseph
Traders : Alexander, C. L.
Date   : 1859/03/12
City   : Memphis   State   : TN

Name   : Joseph
Traders : Miller, John & Mattingly, William
Date   : 1859/10/11
City   : Marion   State   : KY

Name   : Josepher
Traders : Alexander, C. L.
Date   : 1859/03/19
City   : Memphis   State   : TN

Name   : Josephine
Traders : Alexander, C. L.
Date   : 1858/12/04
City   : St. Louis   State   : MO

Name   : Julia
Traders : Alexander, C. L.
Date   : 1859/03/12
City   : Memphis   State   : TN
Note: Julia had a child.

CERTIFICATE FOR SLAVE SALE

Name   : Julia Roach
Traders : Miller, John
Date   : 1858/12/28
City   : Nelson   State : KY

Name   : Kate Martin
Traders : Miller, John
Date   : 1858/12/28
City   : Nelson   State : KY

Name   : Kits
Traders : Hunter, John & Mattingly, William
Date   : 1859/10/04
City   : St. Louis   State : MO

Name   : Kitty
Traders : Alexander, C. L.
Date   : 1858/04/23
City   : St. Louis   State : MO

Name   : Kitty
Traders : Alexander, C. L.
Date   : 1859/03/19
City   : Memphis   State : TN

Name   : Kitty
Traders : McDaniel, Robertson J.
Date   : 1859/11/26
City   : St. Louis   State : MO

Name   : Larry
Traders : Alexander, C. L.
Date   : 1858/04/23
City   : St. Louis   State : MO

Name   : Laura
Traders : Hunter, John & Mattingly, William
Date   : 1860/01/05
City   : St. Louis   State : MO

Name   : Laura
Traders : McDaniel, Robertson J.
Date   : 1859/11/26

CERTIFICATE FOR SLAVE SALE

Laura(cont)
City   : St. Louis   State   : MO

Name   : Lee
Traders : Hunter, John & Mattingly, William
Date   : 1859/09/21
City   : St. Louis   State   : MO

Name   : Lee
Traders : Hunter, John & Mattingly, William
Date   : 1859/12/06
City   : St. Louis   State   : MO

Name   : Lewis
Traders : Hunter, John & Mattingly, William
Date   : 1859/01/24
City   : St. Louis   State   : MO

Name   : Lewis
Traders : Hunter, John & Mattingly, William
Date   : 1859/09/21
City   : St. Louis   State   : MO

Name   : Lewis
Traders : Hunter, John & Mattingly, William
Date   : 1859/12/06
City   : St. Louis   State   : MO

Name   : Lewis
Traders : Middleton, Anthony
          Stratton, C. M.
          Gloyd, B. F.
Date   : 1860/02/06
City   : Shelby County   State   : KY
Note: Lewis belonged to Adam Maron Middleton.

Name   : Lewis
Traders : Miller, John & Mattingly, William
Date   : 1859/01/14
City   : Nelson County   State   : KY

Name   : Linda
Traders : Hughes, R. D.

CERTIFICATE FOR SLAVE SALE

Linda(cont)
Date   : 1860/09/14
City   : Memphis   State   : TN

Name   : Livey
Traders : Hunter, John & Mattingly, William
Date   : 1859/10/04
City   : St. Louis   State   : MO
Note: Livey had four(4) children.

Name   : Lizz
Traders : Hunter, John & Mattingly, William
Date   : 1859/12/06
City   : St. Louis   State   : MO

Name   : Louisa
Traders : Alexander, C. L.
Date   : 1859/01/08
City   : St. Louis   State   : MO

Name   : Louisa
Traders : Alexander, C. L.
Date   : 1859/03/12
City   : Memphis   State   : TN

Name   : Louisa
Traders : Hughes, R. D.
Date   : 1860/09/14
City   : Memphis   State   : TN

Name   : Lucinda
Traders : Miller, John
Date   : 1860/0829   Age   : 2
City   : Nelson County   State   : KY
Mother : Sarah

Name   : Lucinda
Traders : Sarman, B. F.
Date   : 1859/08/24
City   : St. Louis   State   : MO

Name   : Lucy
Traders : Hunter, John & Mattingly, William

CERTIFICATE FOR SLAVE SALE

Lucy(cont)
Date   : 1859/10/04
City   : St. Louis   State : MO

Name   : Lucy
Traders : McDaniel, Robertson J.
Date   : 1859/11/26
City   : St. Louis   State : MO

Name   : Lucy
Traders : McDaniel, Robertson J.
Date   : 1859/11/26
City   : St. Louis   State : MO

Name   : Ludwell
Traders : Hunter, John & Mattingly, William
Date   : 1859/12/06
City   : St. Louis   State : MO

Name   : Lursa?
Traders : McDaniel, Robertson J.
Date   : 1859/11/26
City   : St. Louis   State : MO

Name   : Mages ?
Traders : Hunter, John & Mattingly, William
Date   : 1859/10/04
City   : St. Louis   State : MO

Name   : Magis
Traders : Hunter, John & Mattingly, William
Date   : 1859/12/06
City   : St. Louis   State : MO

Name   : Mahala
Traders : Miller, John
Date   : 1860/08/29   Age   : 14
City   : Nelson County   State : KY

Name   : Malinda
Traders : Hunter, John & Mattingly, William
Date   : 1859/09/21
City   : St. Louis   State : MO

CERTIFICATE FOR SLAVE SALE

Malinda(cont)
Name   : Manda
Traders : Alexander, C. L.
Date   : 1859/01/24
City   : St. Louis   State : MO

Name   : Manerva
Traders : Hunter, John & Mattingly, William
Date   : 1859/01/24
City   : St. Louis   State : MO

Name   : Manuel
Traders : Hunter, John & Mattingly, William
Date   : 1859/09/21
City   : St. Louis   State : MO

Name   : Maranda
Traders : Hunter, John & Mattingly, William
Date   : 1859/10/04
City   : St. Louis   State : MO

Name   : Margaret
Traders : Alexander, C. L.
Date   : 1859/03/12
City   : Memphis   State : TN

Name   : Margaret
Traders : Hunter, John & Mattingly, William
Date   : 1859/09/21
City   : St. Louis   State : MO

Name   : Margaret
Traders : Miller, John
Date   : 1860/08/29   Age   : 25
City   : Nelson County   State : KY
Children : Jinny and Margaret.

Name   : Margaret
Traders : Miller, John
Date   : 1860/08/29   Age   : 4
City   : Nelson County   State : KY
Mother   : Margaret
Sibling : Jinny

CERTIFICATE FOR SLAVE SALE

```
Name    : Maria
Traders : Hunter, John  & Mattingly, William
Date    : 1859/09/21
City    : St. Louis              State  : MO

Name    : Maria
Traders : Miller, John
Date    : 1860/08/29             Age    : 18
City    : Nelson County          State  : KY

Name    : Maria Ropier
Traders : Miller, John
Date    : 1859/01/31
City    : Nelson                 State  : KY

Name    : Mariah
Traders : Alexander, C. L.
Date    : 1859/03/12
City    : Memphis                State  : TN

Name    : Marion
Traders : Hunter, John  & Mattingly, William
Date    : 1859/01/24
City    : St. Louis              State  : MO

Name    : Martha
Traders : Alexander, C. L.
Date    : 1859/01/24
City    : St. Louis              State  : MO

Name    : Martha
Traders : Huges, R. D.
Date    : 1860/09/14
City    : Memphis                State  : TN

Name    : Martha
Traders : Hunter, John  & Mattingly, William
Date    : 1859/09/21
City    : St. Louis              State  : MO

Name    : Martha
Traders : Miller, John
Date    : 1858/12/28
```

CERTIFICATE FOR SLAVE SALE

Martha(cont)
City   : Nelson   State   : KY

Name   : Martha Ann
Traders : Hunter, John & Mattingly, William
Date   : 1859/09/21
City   : St. Louis   State   : MO

Name   : Mary
Traders : Hunter, John & Mattingly, William
Date   : 1859/10/04
City   : St. Louis   State   : MO

Name   : Mary
Traders : Hunter, John & Mattingly, William
Date   : 1860/01/05
City   : St. Louis   State   : MO

Name   : Mary
Traders : Hunter, John & Mattingly, William
Date   : 1859/01/24
City   : St. Louis   State   : MO

Name   : Mary Jane
Traders : Alexander, C. L.
Date   : 1859/01/24
City   : St. Louis   State   : MO

Name   : Marz
Traders : McDaniel, Robertson J.
Date   : 1859/11/26
City   : St. Louis   State   : MO

Name   : Matilda
Traders : Hunter, John & Mattingly, William
Date   : 1859/12/06
City   : St. Louis   State   : MO

Name   : Matilda
Traders : Hunter, John & Mattingly, William
Date   : 1860/01/05
City   : St. Louis   State   : MO

CERTIFICATE FOR SLAVE SALE

Name   : Matilda
Traders : Hunter, John & Mattingly, William
Date   : 1859/01/24
City   : St. Louis   State   : MO

Name   : Mill
Traders : Hunter, John & Mattingly, William
Date   : 1859/09/21
City   : St. Louis   State   : MO

Name   : Milly
Traders : Hunter, John & Mattingly, William
Date   : 1859/09/21
City   : St. Louis   State   : MO

Name   : Milly
Traders : Hunter, John & Mattingly, William
Date   : 1859/01/24
City   : St. Louis   State   : MO

Name   : Milly
Traders : Alexander, C. L.
Date   : 1859/02/07
City   : St. Louis   State   : MO

Name   : Mose
Traders : Hunter, John & Mattingly, William
Date   : 1859/10/04
City   : St. Louis   State   : MO

Name   : Nacky Nichols
Traders : Miller, John
Date   : 1858/12/28
City   : Nelson   State   : KY

Name   : Nancy
Traders : Alexander, C. L.
Date   : 1859/01/24
City   : St. Louis   State   : MO

Name   : Nat
Traders : Hunter, John & Mattingly, William
Date   : 1859/01/08

CERTIFICATE FOR SLAVE SALE

Nat(cont)
City   : St. Louis   State : MO

Name   : Nat
Traders : Hunter, John & Mattingly, William
Date   : 1859/01/08
City   : St. Louis   State : MO

Name   : Nathan
Traders : Hunter, John & Mattingly, William
Date   : 1859/01/08
City   : St. Louis   State : MO

Name   : Nell
Traders : Hunter, John & Mattingly, William
Date   : 1859/01/24
City   : St. Louis   State : MO

Name   : Nelly
Traders : **Hunter, John** & Mattingly, William
Date   : 1859/12/06
City   : St. Louis   State : MO

Name   : Nelly
Traders : Miller, John M. & Mattingly, William
Date   : 1859/10/11
City   : Marion   State : KY

Name   : Nelson
Traders : Middleton, Anthony
          Stratton, C. M.
          Gloyd, B. F.
Date   : 1860/02/06
City   : Shelby County   State : KY
Note: Nelson belonged to Adam **Maron** Middleton.

Name   : Paschal
Traders : Mobley, Orran
          Deas, Ephraim
Date   : 1859/12/23
City   : Shelby County   State : KY
Note: Paschal belonged to James Myers.

CERTIFICATE FOR SLAVE SALE

Name   : Patey
Traders : Hunter, John & Mattingly, William
Date   : 1859/10/04
City   : St. Louis   State   : MO

Name   : Patsy
Traders : Mobley, Orran
          Deas, Ephraim
Date   : 1859/12/23
City   : Shelby County   State   : KY
Note: Patsy belonged to James Myers.

Name   : Peter
Traders : Hunter, John & Mattingly, William
Date   : 1859/01/24
City   : St. Louis   State   : MO

Name   : Phil
Traders : Alexander, C. L.
Date   : 1859/03/12
City   : Memphis   State   : TN

Name   : Philip
Traders : Alexander, C. L.
Date   : 1859/03/12
City   : Memphis   State   : TN

Name   : Phillis
Traders : Hunter, John & Mattingly, William
Date   : 1859/09/21
City   : St. Louis   State   : MO

Name   : Rachel
Traders : Alexander, C. L.
Date   : 1858/04/23   Age   : 17
City   : St. Louis   State   : MO

Name   : Rasmus
Traders : Hunter, John & Mattingly, William
Date   : 1859/09/21
City   : St. Louis   State   : MO

Name   : Richard

CERTIFICATE FOR SLAVE SALE

Richard(cont)
Traders : Miller, John & Mattingly, William
Date   : 1859/10/11
City   : Marion   State : KY

Name   : Richard Beshears?
Traders : Alexander, C. L.
Date   : 1858/12/04
City   : St. Louis   State : MO

Name   : Robert
Traders : Alexander, C. L.
Date   : 1859/01/08
City   : St. Louis   State : MO

Name   : Robert
Traders : McDaniel, Robertson J.
Date   : 1859/11/26
City   : St. Louis   State : MO

Name   : Rosannah
Traders : Alexander, C. L.
Date   : 1859/01/08
City   : St. Louis   State : MO

Name   : Rounder
Traders : Alexander, C. L.
Date   : 1858/12/04
City   : St. Louis   State : MO

Name   : Sally
Traders : Hunter, John & Mattingly, William
Date   : 1859/09/21
City   : St. Louis   State : MO

Name   : Sally
Traders : McDaniel, Robertson J.
Date   : 1859/11/26
City   : St. Louis   State : MO

Name   : Sally
Traders : Mobley, Orran
          Deas, Ephraim

CERTIFICATE FOR SLAVE SALE

Sally(cont)
Date   : 1859/12/23
City   : Shelby County   State   : KY
Note: Sally belonged to James Myers.

Name   : Sally Ann
Traders : Alexander, C. L.
Date   : 1859/03/12
City   : Memphis   State   : TN

Name   : Sam
Traders : Hunter, John & Mattingly, William
Date   : 1859/01/24
City   : St. Louis   State   : MO

Name   : Sam
Traders : Hunter, John & Mattingly, William
Date   : 1859/12/06
City   : St. Louis   State   : MO

Name   : Sam
Traders : Miller, John & Mattingly, William
Date   : 1859/10/11
City   : Marion   State   : KY

Name   : Sampson
Traders : Alexander, C. L.
Date   : 1859/03/12
City   : Memphis   State   : TN

Name   : Sanford Allen
Traders : Alexander, C. L.
Date   : 1858/12/04
City   : St. Louis   State   : MO

Name   : Sara
Traders : Hunter, John & Mattingly, William
Date   : 1859/09/21
City   : St. Louis   State   : MO

Name   : Sara
Traders : Hunter, John & Mattingly, William
Date   : 1859/09/21

CERTIFICATE FOR SLAVE SALE

Sara (cont)
City   : St. Louis   State   : MO
Note: Sara had a child.

Name   : Sara
Traders : McDaniel, Robertson J.
Date   : 1859/11/26
City   : St. Louis   State   : MO

Name   : Sarah
Traders : Alexander, C. L.
Date   : 1858/04/23
City   : St. Louis   State   : MO

Name   : Sarah
Traders : Huges, R. D.
Date   : 1860/09/14
City   : Memphis   State   : TN

Name   : Sarah
Traders : Hunter, John & Mattingly, William
Date   : 1859/09/21
City   : St. Louis   State   : MO

Name   : Sarah
Traders : Hunter, John
Date   : 1859/03/13
City   : St. Louis   State   : MO

Name   : Sarah
Traders : Miller, John & Mattingly, William
Date   : 1859/10/11
City   : Marion   State   : KY

Name   : Sarah
Traders : Miller, John
Date   : 1860/08/29   Age   : 25
City   : Nelson County   State   : KY
Child   : Lucinda

Name   : Sarsa? Tichnor
Traders : Miller, John
Date   : 1858/12/28

CERTIFICATE FOR SLAVE SALE

Sarsa(cont)
City   : Nelson   State : KY

Name   : Scipio
Traders : Middleton, Anthony
          Stratton, C. M.
          Gloyd, B. F.
Date   : 1860/02/06
City   : Shelby County   State : KY
Note: Scipio belonged to Adam Maron Middleton.

Name   : Scott
Traders : Hunter, John & Mattingly, William
Date   : 1859/10/04
City   : St. Louis   State : MO

Name   : Scuna?
Traders : Hunter, John & Mattingly, William
Date   : 1859/09/21
City   : St. Louis   State : MO

Name   : Sila
Traders : Hunter, John & Mattingly, William
Date   : 1859/01/24
City   : St. Louis   State : MO

Name   : Silva
Traders : Hunter, John & Mattingly, William
Date   : 1859/01/24
City   : St. Louis   State : MO

Name   : Sim
Traders : Jerman
Date   : 1858/01/08
City   : St. Louis   State : MO
Wife   : Henriett
Note: Sim and Henriett had an infant child.

Name   : Sizzy
Traders : Hunter, John & Mattingly, William
Date   : 1859/01/24
City   : St. Louis   State : MO

CERTIFICATE FOR SLAVE SALE

Name   : Smith
Traders : Hunter, John & Mattingly, William
Date   : 1859/09/21
City   : St. Louis   State : MO

Name   : Sofia Carter
Traders : Alexander, C. L.
Date   : 1858/12/04
City   : St. Louis   State : MO

Name   : Soloman
Traders : Alexander, C. L.
Date   : 1859/03/12
City   : Memphis   State : TN

Name   : Solomon
Traders : Alexander, C. L.
Date   : 1859/02/07
City   : St. Louis   State : MO

Name   : Sophey
Traders : Hunter, John & Mattingly, William
Date   : 1859/01/08
City   : St. Louis   State : MO

Name   : Sped?
Traders : Hunter, John & Mattingly, William
Date   : 1859/01/08
City   : St. Louis   State : MO

Name   : Spencer
Traders : McDaniel, Robertson J.
Date   : 1859/11/26
City   : St. Louis   State : MO

Name   : Stephen
Traders : Alexander, C. L.
Date   : 1859/01/08
City   : St. Louis   State : MO

Name   : Stephen
Traders : Hunter, John & Mattingly, William
Date   : 1859/09/21

CERTIFICATE FOR SLAVE SALE

Stephen (cont)
City   : St. Louis   State   : MO

Name   : Steven
Traders : McDaniel, Robertson J.
Date   : 1859/11/26
City   : St. Louis   State   : MO

Name   : Sue Cooper
Traders : Miller, John
Date   : 1858/12/28
City   : Nelson   State   : KY

Name   : Sue Mudd
Traders : Miller, John
Date   : 1858/12/28
City   : Nelson   State   : KY

Name   : Suisa
Traders : Hunter, John
Date   : 1859/01/08
City   : St. Louis   State   : MO

Name   : Susan
Traders : Hunter, John & Mattingly, William
Date   : 1859/10/04
City   : St. Louis   State   : MO

Name   : Taylor
Traders : Hunter, John & Mattingly, William
Date   : 1860/01/05
City   : St. Louis   State   : MO

Name   : Thomas
Traders : Hunter, John & Mattingly, William
Date   : 1859/09/21
City   : St. Louis   State   : MO

Name   : Tom
Traders : Hunter, John & Mattingly, William
Date   : 1859/01/24
City   : St. Louis   State   : MO

CERTIFICATE FOR SLAVE SALE

Name   : Tom
Traders : Hunter, John
Date   : 1859/03/13
City   : St. Louis   State : MO

Name   : Tuor? Ann
Traders : Alexander, C. L.
Date   : 1858/12/04
City   : St. Louis   State : MO

Name   : Tyler
Traders : Sarman, B. F.
Date   : 1859/08/24
City   : St. Louis   State : MO

Name   : Vilot Ann
Traders : Hunter, John & Mattingly, William
Date   : 1859/10/04
City   : St. Louis   State : MO
Note: Vilot Ann had a child.

Name   : Wadius
Traders : Hughes, R. D.
Date   : 1860/09/14
City   : Memphis   State : TN

Name   : Wesly
Traders : Middleton, Anthony & Stratton, C. M.
          Gloyd, B. F.
Date   : 1860/02/06
City   : Shelby County   State : KY
Note: Wesly belonged to Adam Maron Middleton.

Name   : West
Traders : Hunter, John & Mattingly, William
Date   : 1859/10/04
City   : St. Louis   State : MO

Name   : William
Traders : Hunter, John & Mattingly, William
Date   : 1859/09/21
City   : St. Louis   State : MO

CERTIFICATE FOR SLAVE SALE

```
Name    : William
Traders : Hunter, John & Mattingly, William
Date    : 1860/01/05
City    : St. Louis            State : MO

Name    : William
Traders : Hunter, John
Date    : 1859/01/08
City    : St. Louis            State : MO

Name    : William
Traders : Hunter, John & Mattingly, William
Date    : 1859/01/24
City    : St. Louis            State : MO

Name    : William Cooper
Traders : Miller, John
Date    : 1858/12/28
City    : Nelson               State : KY

Name    : William Custy
Traders : Alexander, C. L.
Date    : 1858/12/04
City    : St. Louis            State : MO

Name    : William White
Traders : Alexander, C. L.
Date    : 1858/12/04
City    : St. Louis            State : MO

Name    : Willis
Traders : Hunter, John & Mattingly, William
Date    : 1859/09/21
City    : St. Louis            State : MO

Name    : Willis Lynch
Traders : Alexander, C. L.
Date    : 1858/12/04
City    : St. Louis            State : MO

Name    : Wilson
Traders : Hunter, John
Date    : 1859/01/08
```

CERTIFICATE FOR SLAVE SALE

Wilson(cont)
City   : St. Louis   State : MO

Name   : Winney
Traders : Hunter, John & Mattingly, William
Date   : 1859/01/24
City   : St. Louis   State :MO

Willbook A Witnesses

Witness: Applegate, George   Willname: Thompson, John
Date   : 1833/03/30   Page   : 292

Witness: Archer, James   Willname: Evans, Thomas
Date   : 1813/06/02   Page   : 048

Witness: Baggitt, Harisson   Willname: Mundell, A. H.
Date   : 1813/02/12   Page   : 226

Witness: Barnes, Thomas   Willname: White, Thomas
Date   : 1813/01/16   Page   : 042

Witness: Barns, Dennis   Willname: Thompson, John
Date   : 1833/03/30   Page   : 292

Witness: Bettez, Julias   Wilname : Clark, Gibson
Date   : 1820/02/23   Page   : 226

Witness: Blanton, B.   Willname: Trimble, Watt
Date   : 1832/10/22   Page   : 093

Witness: Bogs, Clemmons   Willname: Manning, Silas
Date   : 1813/05/10   Page   : 046

Witness: Booth, John   Willname: Brokus, William
Date   : 1805/10/05   Page   : 021

Witness: Booth, Shelley   Willname: Gibson, Tobias
Date   : 1803/08/02   Page   : 012

Witness: Brenton, Fanny   Willname: Clarke, Lewis
Date   : 1821/10/30   Page   : 218

Willbook A Witnesses

Witness: Bridger, Samuel
Date   : 1805/12/30
Willname: Brokus, William
Page   : 021

Witness: Brook, Bill
Date   : 1833/03/30
Willname: Thompson, John
Page   : 290

Witness: Burnet, David
Date   : 1805/12/30
Willname: Brokus, William
Page   : 021

Witness: Burnett, Daniel
Date   : 1823/05/24
Willname: Basset, William
Page   : 129

Witness: Burnett, Dan
Date   : 1820/02/23
Willname: Clark, Gibson
Page   : 093

Witness: Burriss, Abram
Date   : 1813/02/09
Willname: Cobun, Samuel
Page   : 045

Witness: Byrd, Latton
Date   : 1823/05/24
Willname: Basset, William
Page   : 129

Witness: Burris, Abrams
Date   : 1813/02/09
Willname: Cobun, Samuel
Page   : 045

Witness: Cade, John
Date   : 1813/02/09
Willname: Cobun, Samuel
Page   : 045

Witness: Campbell, William
Date   : 1813/11/15
Willname: Brashears, Martha
Page   : 059

Witness: Carson, Stephen
Date   : 1814/03/06
Willname: Sparks, R.
Page   : 063

Willbook A Witnesses

Witness: Caston, Seth
Date : 1803/08/02
Willname: Gibson, Tobias
Page : 012

Witness: Choat, Isaac W.
Date : 1832/01/09
Willname: Breazeale, Willis
Page : 261

Witness: Choat, Isaac W.
Date : 1833/05/07
Willname: Breazeale, D. W.
Page : 296

Witness: Churchill, Samuel
Date : 1819/10/29
Willname: Phillips, Jenken
Page : 215

Witness: Clark, J. G.
Date : 1817/11/24
Willname: Gibson, Samuel
Page : 080

Witness: Clark, John H.
Date : 1832/01/08
Willname: Breazeale, Willis
Page : 261

Witness: Clark, Lewis
Date : 1823/09/08
Willname: Clark, Elijah
Page : 134

Witness: Clough, Thomas
Date : 1827/07/31
Willname: Durbin, Daniel
Page : 202

Witness: Cloyd, Sam
Date : 1813/11/15
Willname: Brashears, Martha
Page : 059

Witness: Cobun, John B.
Date : 1816/03/26
Willname: Frazer, Elizabeth
Page : 066

Witness: Cobun, J.B.
Date : 1820/10/25
Willname: Barnes, Abram
Page : 223

Willbook A Witnesses

Witness: Cobun, Kitty
Date   : 1833/05/17
Willname: Bullock, Mary
Page   : 274

Witness: Cobun, Ann
Date   : 1817/11/24
Willname: Gibson, Samuel
Page   : 080

Witness: Cobun, Samuel
Date   : 1824/03/08
Willname: Barnes, Joseph
Page   : 135

Witness: Coldas, Alexander
Date   : 1828/05/27
Willname: Hamilton, Syrus
Page   : 206

Witness: Coleman, James
Date   : 1827/07/31
Willname: Durbin, Daniel
Page   : 202

Witness: Cook, Fielding
Date   : 1826/07/11
Willname: Hanna, James
Page   : 162

Witness: Cooke, George K.
Date   : 1815/03/14
Willname: Sparks, R.
Page   : 063

Witness: Dale, J. H.
Date   : 1833/05/26
Willname: Prescott, Abel
Page   : 268

Witness: Davis, James
Date   : 1827/05/17
Willname: Alston, Philip
Page   : 204

Witness: Dents, Prisey
Date   : 1826/07/11
Willname: Hanna, James
Page   : 162

Witness: Dents, G. R.
Date   : 1826/07/11
Willname: Hanna, James
Page   : 162

Willbook A Witnesses

Witness: Downing, D. D. Willname: Clarke, J. G.
Date   : 1822/05/27   Page   : 205

Witness: Downing, John   Willname: Phillips, Jenken
Date   : 1819/11/29   Page   : 215

Witness: Ervin, James   Willname: Breazeale, Willis
Date   : 1833/01/28   Page   : 261

Witness: Favas, Thomas   Willname: McCaleb, William
Date   : 1813/08/19   Page   : 051

Witness: Ferguson, Joseph Willname: Gibson, Tobias
Date   : 1803/08/02   Page   : 012

Witness: German, Asa   Willname: White, Thomas
Date   : 1813/01/16   Page   : 042

Witness: Gibson, J. B.   Willname: Gibson, Ann
Date   : 1827/09/11   Page   : 215

Witness: Goddard, A.   Willname: Watts, Nancy
Date   : 1831/03/12   Page   : 227

Witness: Grafton, Thomas Willname: Stampley, Jacob
Date   : 1826/06/02   Page   : 165

Witness: Gray, Thomas   Willname: Sparks, R.
Date   : 1814/03/06   Page   : 063

Witness: Greenleaf, Harriet Willname: Gibson, Ann
Date   : 1827/09/11   Page   : 218

Willbook A Witnesses

Witness: Grubles, Lewis
Date : 1830/07/26
Willname: Daniel, Ann
Page : 219

Witness: Hall, Edward
Date : 1833/07/03
Willname: Smith, G. W.
Page : 276

Witness: Harmon, Catherine
Date : 1813/05/10
Willname: Manning, Silas
Page : 046

Witness: Hays, John
Date : 1833/01/28
Willname: Breazeale, Willis
Page : 261

Witness: Henson, John
Date : 1832/04/18
Willname: Brisco, Thomas
Page : 232

Witness: Hill, Brook
Date : 1833/03/30
Willname: Thompson, John
Page : 292

Witness: Johnston, John
Date : 1821/10/30
Willname: Clarke, Lewis
Page : 207

Witness: Lyon, Peter
Date : 1813/01/16
Willname: White, Thomas
Page : 042

Witness: Manning, Urilla
Date : 1828/05/25
Willname: White, Joseph
Page : 205

Witness: McCarry, Ed
Date : 1831/03/13
Willname: Trimble, Watt
Page : 233

Witness: McDonald, William
Date : 1833/04/13
Willname: Brashears, J. B.
Page : 280

Willbook A Witnesses

Witness: Minor, W.B. Willname: Evans, Thomas
Date   : 1813/06/18 Page   : 048

Witness: Mison, James Willname: Brashears, J. B.
Date   : 1833/04/13 Page   : 280

Witness: Montgomery, G. W. Willname: Smith, G.M.
Date   : 1833/07/03 Page   : 276

Witness: Moore, Jack Willname: Ross, Sarah
Date   : 1806/07/30 Page   : 023

Witness: Murdock, Francis Willname: Brashears, J.B.
Date   : 1833/05/13 Page   : 280

Witness: Newton, B. Willname: Crane, Waterman
Date   : 1823/02/05 Page   : 151

Witness: Offritt, Fielder Willname: Clarke, J. G.
Date   : 1822/05/27 Page   : 205

Witness: Ogdun, Ellas Willname: Brisco, Thomas
Date   : 1832/04/18 Page   : 232

Witness: Pakery, James P. Willname: Bullock, Mary
Date   : 1833/05/17 Page   : 214

Witness: Powers, Isaac Willname: Daniel, Ann
Date   : 1827/09/11 Page   : 218

Witness: Mirch, James Willname: Prescott, Abel
Date   : 1833/05/26 Page   : 268

Willbook A Witnesses

Witness:	Pugh, John	Willname:	Prescott, Abel
Date	: 1833/05/26	Page	: 268
Witness:	Ragsdale, Edward	Willname:	Daniel, Ann
Date	: 1830/07/26	Page	: 219
Witness:	Robertson, John	Willname:	Clarke, Lewis
Date	: 1821/10/30	Page	: 207
Witness:	Robertson, John	Willname:	Evans, Thomas
Date	: 1813/06/18	Page	: 048
Witness:	Robertson, John	Willname:	White, Joseph
Date	: 1828/05/25	Page	: 205
Witness:	Ross, Charles H.	Willname:	Cobun, Samuel
Date	: 1813/02/09	Page	: 045
Witness:	Ross, Nimrod	Willname:	Ross, Sarah
Date	: 1806/07/30	Page	: 023
Witness:	Shields, Benjamin	Willname:	Hill, Lucy
Date	: 1830/08/20	Page	: 234
Witness:	Simms, James	Willname:	Alston, Phillip
Date	: 1827/05/17	Page	: 204
Witness:	Simms, William	Willname:	Alston, Phillip
Date	: 1827/05/17	Page	: 204
Witness:	Simpson, James	Willname:	Ross, Sarah
Date	: 1806/07/30	Page	: 023

Willbook A Witnesses

Witness: Slaughter, John Willname: Foster, William
Date   : 1812/02/10   Page   : 039

Witness: Stampley, John   Willname: Stampley, Jacob
Date   : 1826/06/02   Page   : 165

Witness: Terry, William   Willname: Prince, Bayliss
Date   : ????   Page   : 148

Witness: Warren, J. B.   Willname: Brisco, Thomas
Date   : 1832/04/18   Page   : 232

Witness: Watson, James   Willname: Cotton, Thomas
Date   : 1829/07/01   Page   : 230

Witness: White, Joel   Willname: Ritchey, Daniel
Date   : 1813/04/14   Page   : 049

Witness: White, Thomas   Willname: Brokus, William
Date   : 1805/12/30   Page   : 021

Witness: Whiting, Amos   Willname: Clarke, J. G.
Date   : 1822/05/27   Page   : 205

Witness: Wilkinson, A.   Willname: Crane, Waterman
Date   : 1826/02/05   Page   : 151

Witness: Williams, James Willname: Phillips, Jenken
Date   : 1819/11/29   Page   : 215

Witness: Williams, John   Willname: McCaleb, William
Date   : 1813/08/09   Page   : 051

Willbook A Witnesses

Witness:	Willis, Daniel	Willname:	Barnes, Abram
Date	: 1830/10/25	Page	: 223
Witness:	Wiseman, Davenport	Willname:	Ritchey, Dan
Date	: 1813/04/18	Page	: 049
Witness:	Young, Clarissa	Willname:	Hill, Lucy
Date	: 1830/08/20	Page	: 234
Witness:	Young, William	Willname:	Hill, Lucy
Date	: 1830/08/30	Page	: 234

WillBook A Additional
Names

Chambliss, William
Clavit, James
Clarke, Joshua
Davis, Reuben
Douglass, James
Daniell, Smith
Eskridge, Thomas P.
Evans, George
Evans, W.C.
Faulk, Orean
Flower, Elisha
Flower, Nancy
Foscue, Lewis
Foster, Gibson
Frazer, Elipth
Gibson, Will
Goodwin, Samuel
Gordor, Adam
Irish, George
Hampton, Darius
Hamilton, Cyrus
Harmon, Janus
Henderson, William
Hill, Lucy Ann
Hobert, Z.B.
Jennings, John
Jones, John
Jones, George
Jones, Susanna
King, William
Knowlton, John
Lane, William
Lim, Erasters
Livingson, T.V.B.
McAlister, H.
McAlphine, Alexander
McElivse, James
McFarland, Davis
Miller, William
Minor, J.B.
Moore, Jeff
Moore, Joseph Dr
Murdock, John

Patterson, Joseph
Powers, Polly
Prince, B. E.
Ragsdale, Edward
Ross, Isaac
Ross, John
Rhodes, Tholemiah
Sale, P. B.
Scott, John
Shields, Benjamin
Sim, James
Simonds, Ephriam
Singleton, John G.
Smith, Cheleab
Smith, G.M.
Smith, Gibson
Swords, Archibald
Trimble, Walter
Townsley, Robert
Vandorn, P. A.
Vause, Thomas
Wallace, David
Waters, Arnold E.
Webster, George W.
White, Larken
White, Rueben
Wilcox, Preston B.
Wills, William
Willis, Esther A.
Willis, William
Wilson, Ava
Wiseman, D.
Wych, William H.

INDEX

AARON, 53-55 59 64 67 92 93
  105 113 115
ABELL, 125
ABNER, 53
ABRAHAM, 1 53
ABRAM, 1-3 7 9 14-16 22 26-30
  32 38 43 47 49 51 53 56 59
  69 76 83 85 103 119 123 169
  170 177
ABSALOM, 53 60 74 77 100 106
  112
ADALINE, 53 125
ADAM, 1 53 125 131 150 157 162
  165 178
ADELAIDE, 53 54 62
ADELE, 54
ADELINE, 125
AFFEY, 1
AGGY, 2 54
AGNES, 125 126
AGNEZ, 125
AILSEY, 54
ALBERT, 2 7 53 54 73 84 85 94
  113 115 122
ALEX, 125
ALEXANDER, 2 6 15 22 32 35 36
  42 45 49 51 53 54 62 63 66
  83 97 113 115 120 126 127
  129 136 138 149 151 153-156
  158-161 163 165 166 171 178
ALEXANDER, C.L. 126 127 129-
  136 138-149 151 153-156
  158-161 163 165 166
ALFORD, 125
ALFRED, 2 54 126
ALICE, 54 55 57 62 92 103

ALICK, 126
ALLEN, 2 31 46 55 160
ALLEN, Dan 31
ALLIACE, 126
ALLICE, 55
ALLICK, 55
ALLIS, 55 96 97
ALLY, 2
ALNISA, 55
ALPHNEA, 3
AMANDA, 55 125 126 140
AMELIA, 2 3 5 11-13 16 22 25
  29 30 43 48 56
AMERICA, 126 127
AMERICUS, 56
AMIOS, 127
AMOS, 56 60 64 83 103 110 176
AMUS, 56
AMY, 56 66 127
ANDERSON, 3 40 56
ANDERSON, Clarinda 40
ANDREW, 14 15 38 42 49 55-57
  62 92 103 127
ANGELINE, 127
ANN, 1-3 5 9 10 13-17 23 26 27
  31 32 38 39 42 44 46 47 49
  50 53 56-65 67 69 71 72 75
  76 80-82 84 86 87 90 93 96
  97 98-104 106-114 116-123
  127 128 136 155 160 165
  171-175 178
ANNACE, 3
ANNEY, 3
ANTHONY, 58 131 150 157 162
  165
ANTONY, 128

INDEX

APPLEGATE, George 168
ARAB, 3 4
ARCH, 58
ARCHER, James 168
ARENA, 4
AREODINE, 58
ARIANN, 4
ARISTIDE, 4
ARMSTED, 4
ARNETTE, 58
ARNOLD, 58 178
ARRILLA, 128
ARTHUR, 129
ARUELIA, 58 59 67 69 74 89 111
AUGUSTUS, 5 7 36 41 50 59
AUSTIN, 59
BAGGITT, Harisson 168
BARBARA, 129
BARNES, Abram 22 29
BARNES, Elias 1 6 15 18 19 22 29 33 39 43 50 52
BARNES, Esther 6 11 14 15 18 19 22 29 39 43 50 52
BARNES, Hariett 11
BARNES, Harriet 8 29
BARNES, Joseph 4 8 29 34 37 39 44 46 47
BARNES, Mary 37
BARNES, Sarah 35 39 44 47
BARNES, Susan 4 37 46
BARNES, Thomas 6 37 168
BARNES, Esther 1
BARNS, Dennis 168
BARRY, 129
BASSET, William 22
BASSETT, 6 8 30 37 40
BASSETT, Huston 30 40
BATTEES, 129
BECCA, 59
BECK, 4
BEIN, 129
BEN, 4 59 129
BENN, 129
BENTON, 129 130
BERRY, Ellen A. 79 90
BESS, 59 130
BETH, 4
BETS, 59
BETSEY, 59 60 109 116
BETSY, 46 8 56 60 64 71 83 88 94 103 110 118 122
BETTA, 5 21
BETTEZ, Julias 168
BETTY, 5 130
BIDDY, 60
BILL, 57 22 26 35 51 60 61 74 93 104 112 113 122 130 169
BILLY, 2 6 15 22 32 35 36 42 45 49 51 61 94 116
BLACK, Napoleon 32
BLAND, Emeline 54 56 58 61 68 74 76 79 85 86 88 89 91 95 105 107 108 110 111 117 122 123
BLANTON, B 168
BOATSWAIN, 6
BOB, 6 7 61 130
BOBO, Eliza M 60 74 112
BOGS, Clemmons 168
BOOTH, John 168
BOOTH, Shelley 168
BRAIM, 62
BRASHEARS, 13 59 11-13 16 17 20-22 25-27 29 30 33 35-38 40-44 46-48 50 169 170 173 174
BRASHEARS, Amelia 2 3 5 11-13 16 22 25 29 30 43 48
BRASHEARS, Catherine 30
BRASHEARS, Jane 21
BRASHEARS, Joseph 3 6 8 17 21 26 35-38 42 46 47
BRASHEARS, Lea 46 50
BRASHEARS, Marsham 25 41
BRASHEARS, Tobias 20 29
BRASHEARS, Turner 5 7 9 13 17 25 27 33 41 43 44 48
BRASHEARS, Joseph 7
BRASHEARS, Priscilla 11 47
BREASHEARS, Joseph 1
BREAZEALE, 31 46 170 172 173
BREAZEALE, Mary 46
BRENTON, Fanny 168
BREWER, 7

INDEX 183

BREDGER, Samuel 169
BRINTON, Piety 28
BRISCO, 33
BRISCO, Claiborne 1 7 9 12 24 45
BRISCO, Thomas 1 4 7 9 10 12 18 24 27 32 33 37 45
BRISCO, Twilland 4 18 28 32 33
BRISCO, Virly 10 37
BROCK, Vashti 55 60 65 68 72 73 80 82 87 93 96 97 100 104 113 114 117
BROKUS, Ann 10 15 31 38 39 47 50
BROKUS, William 15
BROOK, Bill 169
BROWN, Ann 56 57 59-61 63 65 71 75 76 80 82 84 86 87 90 93 96-98 100 101 106-108 110 111 113 114 116-118 120 121 123
BUCK, 7 54 55 57 60-62 67 70 74 76 78 80 82 84 87 90 92 94 96 103 104 106 108 110 114 117 118 122
BUCK, Maria 54 57 60 61 67 70 74 76 78 80 82 84 87 90 92 94 96 104 106 108 110 114 117 118 122
BULLOCK, Mary 2 6 10 15 22 32 35 36 42 45 49 51
BURDIE, 54 62
BURNET, David 169
BURNETT, Dan 169
BURNETT, Daniel 169
BURR, 6 7 22 26 35 51
BURRIS, Abrams 169
BURRISS, Abram 169
BYRD, Latton 169
CADE, John 169
CAEZAR, 131
CAFFERG, Jefferson 20 28
CAFFERG, John 47
CAFFERG, Mary 20 28 46 47
CALEB, 7 62
CALVIN, 62 63 85 99 114 121 124

CAMILLEO, 62
CARIGO?, 7
CAROLINE, 5 8 9 30 54 56 57 60-64 66 70 71 76 79 83 84 86 92 93 97 98 101 103-105 109 112 121 122 131
CARROL, 63
CARROLL, 63
CARSON, Stephen 169
CARTER, 63 163
CASEY, 7
CASSANDRA, 8
CASTON, Seth 170
CATHARINE, 53 56 58 63 64 66 67 69 70 72-74 79 89 94 99 102 104 106 107 109 113 115 116 117 119 123 131
CATO, 8 64
CATREHEAD, Thebe 34
CATY, 8 64
CEASAR, 64
CELIA, 8
CELY, 56 60 64 71 83 103 110 122
CETTY, 64
CHAMBLISS, Elizabeth 57 61
CHAMBLISS, Mary 62 63 85 99 114 121 124
CHAMBLISS, William 178
CHAN, 8
CHANA, 8 9
CHANEY, 64 67 81 109
CHANY, 64 68
CHAPURNUR, 65 68 73 104 114
CHARITY, 65 82 121 123 131
CHARLES, 3 9-11 23 26 31 32 45 53 56 58 63 65 66 75 83 87 90 94 98 101 120 131 132 175
CHARLEY, 132
CHARLIE, 132
CHARLOTTE, 10 11 21 26 45 49 56 66 132
CHAROLOTTE, 10 101 104
CHOAT, Isaac W 170
CHRISTIAN, 66
CHRISTIE, Caroline 5

INDEX

CHURCHILL, Samuel 170
CLABON, Harris 10 12 13 15 16 19 23 25 30 31 38 39 46
CLABON, Henderson 15 19 23 25 30 31 39 46
CLABON, Melvina 10 12 13 16 25 38
CLAIBORNE, 1 7 9 12 24 45 60 67 74
CLARA, 11 132
CLARISA, 11 67
CLARISSA, 2 24 51 58 67 68 71 79 84 85 87 88 98 101 109 119 121 132 177
CLARK, Elijah 1
CLARK, Gibson 1 4 8-9 12 14 20 22 38 41
CLARK, J.G. 170
CLARK, John H 170
CLARK, Lewis 170
CLARK, Susanah 4 20 38
CLARKE, Lewis 28 41 42
CLARKE, Martha 55 58 65 69 71 78 82 86 90 91 95 97 109 112 113 115 118 119 123 124
CLARKEY?, 11
CLAVITT, James 178
CLEA, 67
CLEM, 64 67 81 109
CLEONE, 67
CLIA, 67
CLOUGH, Thomas 170
CLOYD, Sam 170
COBUN, Ann 171
COBUN, J.B. 170
COBUN, John 8 17 48 170
COBUN, John B 170
COBUN, Kitty 171
COBUN, Samuel 8 17 48 171
COLDAS, Alexander 171
COLEMAN, Catharine 53 56 58 66 67 69 70 72 74 79 89 94 99 104 106 107 109 113 115-117 119 123
COLEMAN, James 171
CONNY, 67 78 81
COOK, Fielding 171

CORA, 59 67 69 74 89 111
CORNEAL, 132
COURTNEY, 65 67 68 72 73 80 100 104 114
CRACK, 68 77 85 99 115 120
CRANE, 2 3 5 9 11-14 16-20 23 24 27 28 30 31 32-36 40 43-45 47-51 174 176
CRANE, Catherine 3 9 13 18 20 23 31 32 40 43 45 48 49 51
CRANE, Elizabeth 24
CRANE, James 19 23 35
CRANE, Waterman 2 3 5 9 11-14 16-20 23 24 27
CRANE, Wiliam 45
CRANE, Catherine 31
CREASY, 68
CROCKETT, 54 68 73 84 85 94 122 132 133
CUFF, 68
CYNTH, 68
CYNTHA, 68
CYNTHIA, 59 64 67 69 74 89 111
CYNTHY, 69
CYRUS, 56 69 103 104 119 123 178
DABNEY, 69
DAFNEY, 69
DAN ALLEN, 31 46
DANIEL, 1-5 8 10 13 17 19 24 30 32-34 36 37 41 42 44 45 49 69 75 91 97 102 116 133 169-171 173-177
DANIEL, Ann 1 2 13 17 49
DANIEL, William 17
DANKEYS, 133
DARCUS, 69
DAVID, 10 11 23 26 45 48 133 169 178
DAVIDSON, Sarah 62 77 90 100
DAVIS, Betsy 6 8
DAVIS, James 171
DAVIS, Sarah 22 40
DEAS, Ephraim 125 137 143 157-159
DECK, Julia Ann 53 62
DELIA, 70

DEMPS, 70
DENNIS, 70 105 168
DENTS, G.R. 171
DIANA, 70 134
DICEY, 70
DICK, 11 16 17 33 36 50 70 79 84 97 98 134
DILCEY, 71
DILEY, 11
DILL, 134
DILLER, 71
DINA, 11 16 17 33 36 50
DINAH, 12 71
DOIL?, 12
DOLL, 12 23
DOLLY, 12 134
DORCUS, 12 134
DOWNING, D.D. 172
DOWNING, John 172
DRAER, Jane 39
DRAKE, 134
DREAER, Jane 25 40
DRUCILLA, 134
DURBIN, Daniel 3-5 8 10 13 17 19 24 30 32-34 36 37 41 42 44 45 49
DURBIN, Elizabeth 1 3-5 8 13 17 19 24 30 32-34 36 37 41 43-45 49
EARLINE, 71
EASTER, 71
EASTON, Ann 42
EASTON, Zacariah 42
EBB, 56 60 64 71 83 103 122
ED, 135 173
EDMOND, 71 135
EDNY, 53 71 77 100 106
EDY, 72 135
ELAM, 2 4 23 31 72
ELENOR, Hamilton's 10 25 28 35 52
ELIAS, Barnes 43 52
ELICK, 135
ELINYSA, 135
ELIZA, 12-14 20 24 27 40 54 60 65 68 72-74 80 84 85 94 96 100 102 104 112 114 122 135

ELIZA (Cont'd) 136
ELIZA JANE, 136
ELIZABETH, 1 3-5 8 9 13 17 19 22 24 30 32-34 36 37 41 43-45 48 49 53 55-59 61 63 64 65-70 72-77 80-83 85 87-89 91-94 99 100 101 103-105 108 111 114 116 119-123 136 170
ELIZABETH ANN, 136
ELLA, 74
ELLEN, 59 60 67 69 74 75 79 89 90 95 103 111 112 136
ELLICK, 75
ELLY, 13
ELSEY, 13 75 97 116
ELVIRA, 75
EMALINE, 75
EMANUEL, 75
EMILY, 13 14 44 55-62 64 66 67 70 72 74-78 81 83 84 88 89 91-93 95 96 99 100 102 103 106-109 111 112 114 117 118 120 121 124 137
EMMELINE, 137
EOSE?, 14
EPHRAIM, 76 125 137 143 157-159
EPHRAM, 14
ERVIN JAMES, 172
ESTHER, 1 6 11 14 15 18 19 22 29 33 39 43 50 52 76 178
EVALINE, 14 49
EVELINE, 14 38 76
FANNEY, 137
FANNY, 14 15 68 76 77 85 99 106 115 120 137 138 168
FANNY?, 15
FAVAS, Thomas 172
FERDINAND, 53 71 77 100 106
FERGUSON, Joseph 172
FERNDALL, 15
FLORA, 2 6 15 22 32 35 36 42 45 49 51 77
FLORENCE, 15
FORBES, Sarah Ann 99 113

INDEX

FORTUNE, 15 77
FOSTER, 1 15 27 34 38 41 44 176 178
FOSTER, Patsy 41
FOSTER, Rebeckah 15 27
FOSTER, Shadrack 44
FOSTER, William 14 15
FOX, 138
FRANCE, 77
FRANCES, 138
FRANCIS, 55 59 61 64 65 68 71 75 76 78 79 81 83 85 89-92 94 96 98 99 101 102 105 107 110 113 114 119 120 122 123 138 174
FRANK, 15 16 77 78 90 100 138 139
FRANKLIN, 78
FRANKY, 78
FREDERICK, 78
FREELAND, Augustus 36 39 41 50
FREELAND, John 24
FREELAND, Thomas 12 15 18 20 21 24 26 34 39 40
FRISBY, Elizabeth 53 55 59 64 67 92 93 105
GAGE, Rosanna 63 78 86 91 115
GARLAND, 78
GEARL, 16
GEORGA, 139
GEORGE, 16 67 68 78 81 110 121 125 126 139 140 168 171 178
GERMAN, Asa 172
GIBSON, 1 4-9 12 14 19-23 26 32 35 38 41 51 79 134 168-172 178
GIBSON, Elizabeth 9 19
GIBSON, J.B. 172
GIBSON, James 8 19
GIBSON, Joshua 6 7 22 26 35 51
GIBSON, Rebecca 1 5 6 21
GIBSON, Samual 1 5-7 21 22 26 35
GIBSON, Tobias 7 12 23 32
GIP, 140
GITTY, 79

GIZO, 140
GODDARD, A 172
GOLDSMITH, 79 84 97 98
GORDON, Candis 67 75 112
GRACE, 11 16 17 33 36 50 79 140
GRACY, 79
GRAFTON, Thomas 172
GRAY, Thomas 172
GREEN, 2 3 7 9 14-16 26-30 32 38 43 47 49 51 79 88 105
GREEN, Abram 2 3 7 9 14-16 26-30 32 38 43 47 49 51
GREEN, Andrew 14 15 29 32 38 43 49
GREEN, Ann 16 26 27 32
GREEN, Martha 2 3 16 30
GREENLEAF, Harriet 172
GRUBLES, Lewis 173
HALL, Edward 173
HAM, 79
HAMER, Amazon 53 56 77 86 92 98 101 107 112 117 120 124
HAMILTON, Lucy 31
HAMP, 79
HAMPSHIRE, 79
HANKERSON, 79
HANNA, 20 24-27 38 140 171
HANNA, James 20 24-27 38 40
HANNA, William 20 24
HARDENIA, 80
HARIET, 55 68 72-74 80 86 100 103 104 112 114 115 124 141
HARIETT BARNES, 11
HARMON, Catherine 173
HARO, 80
HARRIET, 8 16 17 29 54 57 58 63 64 66 67 70 71 72 73 76 78-83 85-89 93 98 101-105 107-110 112 116 117 119 120 122 141 172
HARRIET ANN, 64 67 81 109
HARRIETTE, 81
HARRISON, 17 81 141 142
HARRY, 17 81 142
HARVE, 81
HARVEY, 17

INDEX

HARY, 11 16 17 33 36 50 142
HAY, 17 18 21
HAYS, John 173
HECTOR, 81 82
HEDDRICK, 9
HEN, 12 18
HENDERSON, 15 19 23 25 30 31 39 46 82 178
HENRIETTA, 82
HENRY, 18 58 63 65 66 68 71 79 82-85 87 88 98 101 109 119 121 123 142 143
HENSON, 83 173
HENSON, John 173
HESTER, 55 56 60 64 71 83 103 110 122
HETTA, 83 84
HILL, Brook 173
HILL, Lucy 178
HINDS, 84
HIRAM, 143 144
HOBERT, Z.B. 178
HORACE, 84
HUGES, R.D. 125 126 137 142 154 161
HULDAH, 70 79 84 97 98
HUMPHREYS, 54 68 73 84 85 94 122
HUNTER, Hannah 51
HUNTER, John 125-147 149-167
HUNTER, Mary 41
HUNTER, William 136
IKE, 84 144
INA, 54 68 73 84 85 94 122
INDIANA, 84
INFANT, 9 28 29 68 77 82 85 99 112 128 137 162
INGRAM, Charlotte 21
IRENE, 65 68 73 84 85 94
ISAAC, 3 9 18 19 23 31 32 66 68 77 85 88 99 105 106 115 120 144 170 174 178
ISABEL, 85
ISAM, 19
ISHAM, 85 86
JACK, 19 20 23 86 87 144 174
JACK STEVENSON, 87

JACKS, 87
JACKSON, 87 144
JACOB, 8 10-13 19 20 23 24 26-28 32 34 40 42 45 48 144 172 176
JAKE, 65 87 90 101
JAMES M. Watson, 12 14 16-18 34 36 51
JANE, 15 21 25 39 40 54 60 61 68 73 79 84 85 87 88 94 104 105 116 122 136 145 146 155
JANUARY, 21 66 101 104
JEFF, 88 178
JEFFERSON, 5 20 21 28 88
JEFFREY, 59 69 74 88 89 111
JENKEN, 28 35 41 51 52
JENKINS, Phillips 21
JENNEY, 22
JENNY, 22 89
JEREMY, 6 7 22 26 35 51
JERMAN, 141 162
JERRY, 89
JESSE, 22 65 87 89 90 101
JILES, 146
JIM, 2 6 15 22 23 32 35 36 40 42 45 49 51 77 90 91 100 146
JINNY, 91 146 153
JO, 12 23 146 147
JOE, 3 9 23 31 32 55 57 62 91 92 103 147
JOHN, 3 4 8 13 16-21 23 24 26-29 33 34 36 37 39 40 44 4648 50 53 54 56-58 64 66 67 69-74 77-81 83 86-89 92-95 99-107 109 110 112 113 115-120 122 123 125 126-170 172 173 175 176 178
JOHN PRINCE, 24
JOHNSTON, John 173
JOLOWES, 148
JONES, John 178
JORDAN, 93
JOSEPH, 1 3 4 68 17 21 24 26 29 34-39 42 44 46 47 61 93 101 104 112 122 148 171 172 173 175 178 179

INDEX

JOSEPHER, 148
JOSEPHINE, 73 93 148
JOSH, 93
JOSHUA, 6 7 16 17 21 22 24 26 34 35 38 39 41 51 178
JUDAH, 24
JUDY, 93
JULIA, 25 53 60 62 88 93 94 148 149
JULIAN, 94
JUNIUS, 54 68 84 85 94 122
KATE, 61 94 116 149
KENTUCK, 94
KESIAH, 25
KING WILLIAM, 178
KITS, 149
KITTY, 25 94 149 171
KY, 125 126 128-133 136-162 164-166
LANDER, 25
LANEY, 25
LARKIN, 94
LARRY, 149
LAUDER, 25
LAURA, 25 94 149 150
LAVINE, 95
LAVINIA, 95
LEANDER, 26
LEE, 6 7 22 26 35 51 150
LEOGIS, 26
LEONARD, 95
LETHE, 95
LETTY, 10 11 26 45 49
LEVI, 26 95
LEVING, 26
LEWIS, 26 28 41 42 95 150 168 170 173 175 178
LEXY, 95
LEYBORNE, Mary, 22 29
LIBERIA, 6 22 32 42 45 49 51
LICKEY, 26 27
LINA, 13 20 24 27 40 48
LINDA, 27 45 150 151
LINNY, 27
LITTLETON, 95 96
LIVELY, 96
LIVINGSON, T.V.B. 178

LIZA, 27 50
LIZZ, 151
LOGAN, 96
LORINDA, 96
LOUIS, 27 96 125-167
LOUISA, 27 28 55 79 96 108 109 151
LUCINDA, 28 47 55 96 97 151 161
LUCY, 28 31 63 64 66 70 73 75 79 83 84 97 98 102 116 151 152 175 177 178
LUDWELL, 152
LUNIA, 28
LURSA, 152
LYLE, 29
LYON, Peter 173
MABORN, 98
MAGARET, 98
MAGES, 152
MAGIS, 152
MAHALA, 152
MALINDA, 29 55 59 61 68-71 75 76 78 79 83 85 89 91 92 94 96 98 99 101 102 105 107 110 113 114 119-123 152 153
MANDA, 68 77 85 99 115 120 153
MANERVA, 99 153
MANNING, Urilla 173
MANSON, 29 99
MANUEL, 29 99 153
MARANDA, 153
MARCH, 29 99
MARGARET, 1 53 64 67 69 71 77 78 81 87-89 95 99 100 106 109 110 118 146 153
MARGARET, Snodgrass 110
MARGE, 99
MARIA, 29 54 57 60 61 67 70 74 76 78 80 82 84 87 90 92 94 96 99 100 104 106 108 110 114 117 118 122
MARIA ROPIER, 154
MARIAH, 30 43 49 51 53 65 68 71-73 77 80 100 104 106 114 154
MARION, 125 126 128 137-140

INDEX

MARION (Cont'd)
  144-146 148 154 157 159 160 161
MARK, 30 100
MARMADUKE, 100
MARTHA, 2 3 7 16 20 25 29 30 41 46 47 50 55 58 65 66 69 71 77 78 82 86 90 91 93 95 97 100 101 104 109 112 113 115 118 119 122-124 154 155 169 170
MARTHA ANN, 155
MARY, 2 3 6 8 10 13 15 20 22 23 28-32 35 36 37 41 42 45-47 51 53-57 60-66 69 71 72 73 76 79 83 85 87 90 92 93 95 97 98-104 108 110-115 119-124 134 155 171 174
MARY ANN, 31 46 56 61 69 93 101 103 104 112 119 122 123
MARY JANE, 104 155
MARYE, Mary P 57 61 76 79 92 95 100 108 111
MARZ, 155
MATILDA, 31 65 66 68 72 73 80 100 101 104 114 155 156
MATTINGLY, William 125-167
MAY, 9 15 32
MCALISTER, H 178
MCALPHINE, Alexander 178
MCALPHINE, Harriet 87
MCCALEB, 14 15 44 172 176
MCCALEB, Ann 14 44
MCCALEB, Jane 15
MCCARRY, Ed 173
MCDANIEL, Robertson J 130 137 138 143-145 147 149 152 155 159 161 163 164
MCDONALD, William 173
MCDOUGALL, Susan 75 91 97 102 116
MCELIVSE, James 178
MCFARLAND, Davis 178
MCGILVARY, Mary 53 54 63 66 83 97 113 115 120
MCINTYRE, Emily 55-62 64 66 67 70 72 74-78 81 83 84 88 89

MCINTYRE (Cont'd)
  91-93 95 96 99 100 102 106-109 111 112 114 117 118 120 121 124
MCNEIL, James 18
MCNEIL, Robert 23 24
MELINDA, 2 6 15 22 32 35 36 42 45 49 51
MIDDLETON, Anthony 131 150 157 162 165
MIKE, 79 88 104 105
MILANDA, 32
MILES, 105
MILL, 3 9 23 31 32 156
MILLER, John 125 126 128-133 136-142 144-154 156 157 159 160 161 164 166
MILLER, William 178
MILLY, 32 70 93 105 156
MIMA, 32 105
MINDA, 32
MINERVA, 105
MINGO, 32 33
MINOR, J.B. 178
MINOR, W.B. 174
MIRA, 106 107 111
MISON, James 174
MISSOURI, 106
MISTY, 33
MO, 125-167
MOBLEY, Orran 125 137 143 157-159
MONK, 77 106
MONROE, 53 71 77 100 106
MONTGOMERY, G.W. 174
MOORE, Jack 174
MOORE, Jeff 178
MOORE, Joseph Dr 178 179
MOORE Joseph Dr. 179
MOORS, Elizabeth 22
MOORS, James 19
MOORS, Johil 11
MOORS, Robert 3 9 11 16 19 22 37
MOORS, William 3
MORACIA, 33
MORGAN, 33

INDEX

MORRIS, Ann 49
MOSE, 106 156
MOSES, 11 16 17 33 34 36 50
    106 107 111
MOURNING, 107
MUNDELL, 42 168
MUNDELL, Abijah 42
MURDOCK, Francis 174
MURDOCK, John 178
MYRA, 3 4 107
NACKY, 156
NAD, 34
NANCY, 2 7 9 12 21 26 34 60 74
    106 107 111 156 172 178
NANCY WATTS, 2 7
NAT, 34 156 157
NATHAN, 157
NED, 34 35 103 107 108
NEDI, 6 7 22 26 35 51
NELL, 35 157
NELLY, 35 108 157
NELSON, 35 125 126 128-133
    136-138 140-142 145 146
    147-157 161 162 164 166
NERO, 108
NERO JUNIOR, 108
NEW, 2 6 15 22 32 35 36 42 45
    49 51
NEWTON, B 174
NINA, 35 36
O'YOUNG, 36
OFFRITT, Fielder 174
OGDUN, Ellas 174
OLEVIA, 64 67 81 109
OLIVA, 109
OLMSTEAD, 109
ORRIE, 36
OSCAR, 109
PAKERY, James P 174
PALLIS, 109
PANDORA, 109
PARIS, 96 109
PARK, 56 60 64 71 83 103 109
    110 122
PARTHENA, 110
PASCHAL, 157
PATEY, 158

PATIENCE, 11 16 17 33 36 50
    110
PATSEY, 110
PATSY, 36 41 110 158
PATTERSON, Joseph 178
PATTY, 2 6 15 22 32 35 36 42
    45 49 51
PEGG, 37
PEGGY, 37 110
PELLERAND, 37
PERRY, 10 37
PETER, 37 38 110 158 173
PHEBE, 38
PHEBY, 110 111
PHIL, 38 158
PHILIP, 158 171
PHILL, 38
PHILLIP, 38 39 44 175
PHILLIPS, 10 21 25 28 31 35 41
    51 52 132 146 170 172 176
PHILLIPS, Gabriel 10
PHILLIPS, Sarah 10
PHILLIS, 39 158
PILEEY, 39
PILLOY, 39
PITCHER, 39
PLUMMER, 111
POLLY, 38 39 111 178
POMP, 39
POMPEY, 39 40
POSEY, Sarah 71 85
POSIBA, 40
POWELL, 111
POWERS, Isaac 174
POWERS, Polly 178
PRESCOTT, Abel 27 50
PRINCE, 13 20 24 27 40 48 176
    178
PRINCE, B.E. 178
PRISCILLA, 40 59 67 69 74 111
PRISSEY, 40
PUGH, John 175
PUSS, 111
PYERS, 40
QUINN, Catherine 28 47
RACHAEL, 40 41
RACHEL, 41 42 46 106 107 111

INDEX

RACHEL (Cont'd)
 158
RAGSDALE, Edward 175 178
RALPH, 56 57 59-61 63 65 71 75
 80 82 87 90 93 97 98 100
 101 104 106-114 116 118 120
 121-123
RALPH SR, 112
RAMSEY, 112
RANDELL, 42
RANEY, 60 74 112
RANSOM, 112
RASMUS, 158
RAYMOND, 112
RHODA, 2 6 15 22 32 35 36 42
 45 49 51
RHODES, Tholemiah 178
RHODY, 112
RICHARD, 112 158 159
RIGHT, 42
REVERS, Mary W 64 72 98 102
ROB, 113
ROBERSON, 113
ROBERT, 3 9 11 16 19 22-24 37
 42 43 113 159 178
ROBERT MOOR'S FIANCE, 37
ROBERTSON, John 175
ROBIN, 30 43 49 113
ROBINSON, Ann 2 5 26 27
ROBINSON, Jeremiah 37
ROBINSON, John 21 26
ROBINSON, Mary 92 95 102
ROBINSON, Nancy 21 26
ROBINSON, Seth 6 19
ROSANNAH, 159
ROSE, 53 54 60 113 115
ROSEANN, 113
ROSS, Charles H 175
ROSS, Isaac 178
ROSS, John 178
ROSS, Nimrod 175
ROSSMAN, Hariet 55 74 86 103
 112 115 124
ROUNDER, 159
ROUSH, John 36
RUNDELL, Judith 81 96 106 109
RUSSAL, 43

RUTLAND, 43
SABRA, 43
SALE, P.B. 178
SALINA, 43
SALLY, 14 43-45 54 63 70 80 82
 85 87 90 96 111 114 115 120
 159 160
SALLY ANN, 160
SALUDA, 114
SAM, 44 68 72 73 77 85 99 100
 104 114 115 120 121 160 170
SAMPSON, 160
SAMUAL, 1 5-7 11 17 21-23 26
 35 44 45 48 51
SANDY, 43-45 115
SANFORD, 160
SANTRE, 53 54 113 115
SARA, 160 161
SARAH, 1 2 6 10 11 22 26 27 35
 36 39 40 42 44-47 49 51 53
 57 58 61-65 67-69 71 74-77
 79-81 85 88-90 92 94 97-100
 105 111 113 115-117 119 123
 151 161 174 175
SARAH ANN, 46 99 113
SARAH H, 46
SARINIA, 116
SARMAN B.F. 145 151
SARSA, 161
SASY, 46
SAXON, Joshua 16 17 21 34 38
 39 41
SAXON, Medar 16 18 21
SAXON, Milbourne 38
SAXON, Orville 34
SAXON, Samual 17
SAYER, Harriet B 63 66 70 73
 76 78 81 82 85 86 98 103
 105 108 116 119
SCIPIO, 162
SCOTT, 162 178
SCOTT, John 178
SCUNA, 162
SHADRACK, 44 60 109 116 117
SHAIFER, Clarissa 58 68 71 79
 84 85 87 88 98 101 109 119
 121

INDEX

SHANAHAN, Elizabeth 81 108 122
SHARPER, 46 116 117
SHED, 46
SHIELDS, Benjamin 175 178
SIDNEY, 117
SILA, 162
SILLAH, 46 47
SILLERS, Caroline 56 60 61 64
  66 70 71 79 83 84 93 97 98
  101 103 104 109 112 122
SILOY, 47
SILVA, 11 47 117 162
SILVIA, 117
SIM, 141 162 178
SIMMS, James 175
SIMMS, William 175
SIMON, 117
SIMONDS, Ephriam 178
SIMPSON, James 175
SIMS, Emeline F 66 68 77 85 88
  99 106 115 120
SINA, 47
SINGLETON, John G 178
SIRUS, 47
SIZZY, 162
SLAUGHTER, John 176
SMITH, 14 38 70 163 173 174
  178
SMITH, Cheleab 178
SMITH, G.M. 178
SMITH, Gibson 178
SMITH, Polly 38
SMITH, Sally 14
SMYTH, A 134
SNODGRASS, Margaret 53 64 67
  69 71 77 78 81 87-89 95 100
  106 109 110 118
SOFIA, 163
SOLOMAN, 163
SOLOMON, 28 47 163
SOPHEY, 163
SOPHIA, 3 4 48 60 109 116-118
SOPHY, 48 118
SPARKS, R 4 29
SPARKS, Ruth 429
SPED, 163
SPENCER, 53 57 58 62 63 67 69

SPENCER (Cont'd)
  74 79 88 89 92 98 105 111
  118 123 163
SPENCER, Sarah A 53 57 58 62
  63 67 69 74 79 88 89 92 98
  105 111 123
ST. JOHN, Ellen 95 103
STAMPLEY, David 10 11 23 26 45
  48
STAMPLEY, Jacob 8 10-12 19 23
STAMPLEY, James 19 23
STAMPLEY, John 176
STAMPLEY, Mary U 8 28
STAMPLEY, Nancy C 12 34
STAMPLEY, Sarah 27 42 45
STAMPS, Jane 54 61 68 73 84 85
  94 116 122
STEPHEN, 48 118 163 164 169
STEVEN, 164
STRATTON, C.M. 131 150 157 162
  165
SUE, 13 20 24 27 40 48 164
SUISA, 164
SUSAN, 4 37 46 48 75 91 97 102
  115 116 118 119 164
SUSEY, 10 11 26 45 48 49
SUTT, 119
SUZETTE, 56 69 103 104 119 123
SWORDS, Archibald 178
SYLVA, 68 77 85 99 115 119 120
TABITHA, 120
TAINEY, 49
TANEY, 49
TARLETON, 14 49
TASWELL, 120
TAYLOR, 13 164
TAYLOR, Mary 13
THEATHA, Eliza 14
TEANER, 120
TEBO, Ann C 75 119
TEMPE, 120
TENA, 120
TENACH, 2 6 15 22 32 35 36 42
  45 49 51
TENNER, 120
TENNESSEE, 120
TERESA CAROLINE MCGIRTY, 9

INDEX

TERRY, William 176
THOMAS, 1 4 6 7 9 10 12 15 18
   20 24 26 27 32-35 37 39 40
   45 49 55-68 70-72 74 75-84
   86-93 95-102 106-114 116-
   118 120 121 123 124 164 168
   170 172-176 178
THOMAS, Sarah 35
THOMPSON, John 3 4 16 18-20 23
   28 29 33 34 37 39 44 48 50
THOMPSON, Myra 3 4
THOMPSON, Sophia 3 4
THOMSON, Caroline 54 57 62 70
   76 92 103 105 121
THOMSON, Elizabeth 70 83 89
   101 116
TILDA, 120
TILLIS, 120
TIURBO, 50
TN, 125 126 130 131 134 135
   137-139 141 142 144 145
   147-149 151 153 154 158 160
   161 163 165
TOM, 27 50 76 121 164 165
TONY, 121
TORA, 11 16 17 33 36 50 51
TOWNSLEY, Robert 178
TRIMBLE, Walter 178
TUGG, Margaret 1
TUOR, Ann, 165
TYLER, 165
VAN BUREN, 61 93 101 104 121
   122
VANDORN, P.A. 178
VAUSE, Thomas 178
VICTORIA, 54 68 73 84 85 94
   122
VILOT ANN, 165
VINCENT, 6 7 22 26 35 51
VING, 122
VIOLET, 51 122
VIRA, 2 6 15 22 32 35 36 42 49
   51
WADIUS, 165
WALKER, Rachel 46
WALLACE, David 178
WARREN, J B 176

WASH, 56 60 64 71 83 103 110
   122
WASHINGTON, 30 43 49 51 122
WATERS, Arnold E 178
WATKINS, Lary 2
WATSON, James 11 12 16-18 33
   36 50 176
WATSON, James M 11 12 16-18 33
   36 50
WATTS, Nancy 2 7
WEBSTER, George W 178
WELLS, 51
WESLEY, 122
WEST, 165
WHITE, Joel 176
WHITE, Larken 178
WHITE, Rueben 178
WHITE, Sarah 1
WHITE, Thomas 1 35 176
WHITING, Amos 176
WILCOX, Preston B 178
WILDA, 122 123
WILKINSON, A 176
WILL, 52 123 178
WILLIAM, 3 6 8 11 12 14-18 20
   22 24 27 30 31 34 36-41 44
   45 47 50 51 54-58 60 61 63
   64 66 67 69-71 73-76 78-87
   90-98 101 103-106 108-120
   122 123 125-169 172 173
   175-178
WILLIAMS, James 176
WILLIAMS, John 176
WILLIS, 31 46 65 82 121 123
   124 166 170 172 173 177 178
WILLIS, Daniel 177
WILLIS, Esther A 178
WILLIS, William 178
WILLOBY, 124
WILLS, William 178
WILSON, 53 56 58 75 87 94 120
   124 166 167 178
WILSON, Elizabeth 53 56 58 75
   87 94 120
WINNEY, 167
WINNY, 124
WISEMAN, D 178

INDEX

WISEMAN, Davenport 177
WLLIAM, 124
WOOLDRIDGE, Elam 2 4 23 31
WOOLDRIDGE, W.H. 2 4
WYCH, William H 178
YENAH, 52
YORK, 124
YOUNG, Clarissa 2 24 51 177
YOUNG, William 177
ZILEAN, 124

BIBLIOGRAPHY

UNPUBLISHED DOCUMENTS

Claiborne County Willbook A

Port Gibson Property List 1846-1858

Certificate of Slaves For Sale (contained in the Port Gibson

Property List 1846-1858)

PUBLISHED

Dunbar, Rowland, "Mississippi, The Heart of the South",
J.J. Clarke Publishing Co., 1923

Warton, Vernon Lane, "The Negro in Mississippi 1865-1890",
Greenwood Press, Westport, CN., 1984